Traces of the Old, Uses of the New

EDITORIAL THEORY AND LITERARY CRITICISM
George Bornstein, Series Editor

Traces of the Old, Uses of the New

The Emergence of Digital Literary Studies

AMY E. EARHART

UNIVERSITY OF MICHIGAN PRESS

ANN ARBOR

Published in the United States of America by the
University of Michigan Press
Printed and bound by CPI Group (UK) Ltd, Croydon, CR0 4YY

2018   2017   2016   2015   4   3   2   1

A CIP catalog record for this book is available from the British Library.

DOI: http://dx.doi.org/10.3998/etlc.13455322.0001.001

ISBN 978-0-472-07278-1 (hardcover : alk. paper)
ISBN 978-0-472-05278-3 (cloth : alk. paper)
ISBN 978-0-472-12131-1 (e-book)

For my family. You are what matters.

Acknowledgments

Without Jerome ("Jerry") McGann and NINES, I would never have become a digital humanist. I was toiling as a lecturer when I was accepted to attend the very first NINES digital workshop in 2005. There I met a group of scholars who inspired me to delve into what was (and is still, unfortunately) a very risky area of scholarly inquiry, digital humanities. Jerry McGann, Bethany Nowviskie, Nick Laiacona, Dana Wheeles, Melissa White, and others involved with University of Virginia's digital renaissance would continue to provide inspiration and support. The workshop participants were equally important to my interest in digital humanities: Stephanie Browner, Gavin Budge, Dennis Denisoff, Neil Fraistat, Susan Garfinkel, David Hanson, Jurretta Jordan Heckscher, Lorraine Janzen, Steven E. Jones, Tim Killick, David Latané, Laura Mandell, James Mussell, Suzanne Paylor, Julia Thomas, and Edward Whitley. I am also fortunate to have had the opportunity to work with Kenneth Price, who has become an invaluable mentor. A professor at Texas A&M University when I was a graduate student, Ken continued to offer suggestions and help as he changed jobs and eventually built a digital humanities powerhouse at the University of Nebraska. Each of these scholars and many, many generous digital humanities scholars around the globe have offered suggestions and encouragement throughout my career and during this project. I have been fortunate to work within a community to which I truly felt I belonged.

I am indebted to the Program to Enhance Scholarly and Creative Activities; the Initiative for Digital Humanities, Media, and Culture (IDHMC), formerly the Digital Humanities Program; and The Melbern G. Glasscock Center for Humanities Research, all at Texas A&M University, for supporting my book. A special thank you to my department heads during this project, Jimmie Killingsworth, Paul Parish, and Nancy Warren, and to my department who decided to hire a digital humanist. I'm sure they are still wondering why they agreed to such a crazy thing. Others who were invaluable to this project and to my sanity include my long-standing colleague and friend Maura Ives, my coconspirator in much of the digital humanities work at Texas A&M University and a great lunch buddy; Jim Harner, an academic mentor, scholarly inspiration, and my go-to source for restaurant recommendations; and our new director of the IDHMC, Laura Mandell. My readers offered very useful suggestions for revision, and the editors at the University of Michigan Press, Tom Dwyer, Aaron McCollough, and Christopher Dreyer, provided invaluable help throughout the process.

My greatest thanks goes to my family, without whom none of this would have been possible. My mother, Marianne Earhart Banks, and my late father, J Ronald Earhart, who always told me that I could. Thank you especially to my husband, Bruce Herbert, who always asks the difficult question, who always knows that I am able, and who agreed to move to a ranch and start a sheep flock. I'm thinking about chickens and guinea hens now, okay? To my daughter, who never thought it was strange when her mother was madly typing on the computer during her swim practices, who occasionally missed meets for work related trips, and who is still proud of her Momma for writing a book (even though she is a teenager).

Contents

Contents

Introduction

Digital Literary Studies in the United States

> It was also interesting to see, during the convention and after, a debate among the Twitter crowd about the label "digital humanities" and whether it was accurate or useful and how to get humanists, digital and otherwise, to talk more (or more usefully) to one another. A catchall phrase comes in handy—it's hard to imagine the NEH's establishing an Office of Cool Scholarship Done With Digital Tools—but it doesn't do justice to the very different kinds of work done under that label. Maybe the term is just a placeholder, and the day is not far off when people won't feel the need to make a distinction between the humanities and the digital humanities.
>
> —Jennifer Howard, "The MLA Convention in Translation," *The Chronicle of Higher Education,* December 31, 2009

Scholars who self define as digital humanists joke that any public discussion on digital humanities will inevitably turn to the question: "What are the digital humanities?" Digital humanists spend what seems to be an inordinate amount of time discussing, defining, and explaining what, in many ways, is an amorphous, fluid area of study. Books, articles, blog posts, tweets, conferences, and conference papers that define "digital humanities" have grown ex-

ponentially, and so common is the query that Matthew Kirschenbaum has called such "what is" essays "genre pieces."[1] While the
digital humanities as an area of scholarly inquiry might appear to
be a recent invention, utilizing computing technology to answer
humanistic questions is often dated to 1946 and Father Busa's *Index Thomisticus*, a concordance program.[2] Early digital work was
conducted on mainframe computers using punch cards or paper
tape and focused on concordance development, authorship studies, and linguistic analysis. As digital technology applications for
humanities materials developed in the 1980s and 1990s, driven in
large part by increased use of microcomputing and the emergence
of the World Wide Web, scholars adopted the term humanities
computing to describe their work. By the early 1990s, humanities computing was well established with growing numbers of
humanities computing departments, centers and institutes, specialized journals, an annual conference, and three distinct scholarly organizations: the Association for Literary and Linguistic
Computing, the Association for Computers and the Humanities, and the Society for Digital Humanities/Société pour l'étude
des médias interactifs. Focused on "information technology as a
tool and written texts as a primary object of study (for linguistic
analysis),"[3] according to Patrik Svenson, humanities computing
was a cohesive scholarly pursuit. The World Wide Web (web or
WWW), however, would change everything and set the stage for
the current tensions in the field. In her comprehensive history of
humanities computing, Susan Hockey argues that at the onset of
the web, "some long-term humanities computing practitioners
had problems in grasping the likely impact of the Web in much
the same way as Microsoft did."[4] In Hockey's analysis, scholars
saw the web as a space devoid of serious activity and unable to
support scholarship, but she also, and perhaps more importantly,
predicts the fissures in humanities computing that would explode
in contemporary conflict. Instead of ensuring a cohesive humanities computing community, who shared a good deal of agreement

on technique and methodology, the web spurred a new set of us-ers who exploited the web's flexibility and openness to diversify scholarly questions and methodologies, often viewed as a direct assault on scholarly rigor and exclusiveness.

By the mid-2000s, humanities computing was declining as a term of choice, with Willard McCarty's *Humanities Computing*, published in 2005, signaling the last substantive use of the term.[5] During the same year, the Association for Literary and Linguis-tic Computing, the Association for Computers and the Humani-ties, and the Society for Digital Humanities/Société pour l'étude des médias interactifs merged into the Alliance of Digital Hu-manities Organizations (ADHO), and humanities computing be-came digital humanities (DH), the term that John Unsworth had coined for the 2004 *Blackwell Companion to Digital Humanities*.[6] Regardless of the acceptance and use of the term digital humani-ties, a working definition remains elusive even to those that call themselves digital humanists. It is not clear whether the digital humanities are a field, a technique, or a trend, or if such defini-tions are antithetical to the scholarly project. Scholars argue over whether the digital humanities should emphasize digital building or theorizing and contest hack versus yack. The metaphor of the big tent, where all those interested in scholarly uses of technol-ogy might reside, continues to be a point of contention, leaving some, such as Matthew Kirschenbaum, to see the term digital humanities as tactical rather than informational.[7]

This book is written as the digital humanities become increas-ingly visible, with articles about DH appearing in the *Chronicle of Higher Education*, increasing numbers of jobs posted in the MLA job list, and a growing number of DH centers across the United States. Yet at disciplinary conferences, college and university meetings, in social media, and in trade publications, such as *Inside Higher Ed*, the "what is DH" question continues to be voiced. This monograph does not seek to provide one definition of digi-tal humanities. Instead, the project suggests that digital humanities is, in many ways, a living term, ever evolving, ever shifting in response to particular pressures of scholarship, the academy, and the individual. Accordingly, the project traces the various theoretical and methodological branches of literary digital humanities to reveal how seemingly unrelated literary movements have shaped current digital humanities practice. Many of the early books on digital humanities have focused on the breadth of the digital humanities, arguing that digital humanities is an inclusive form that is able to be all to all fields. While such a tactic serves the political purpose of making digital humanities indispensable, it obscures the impact of practitioners from various disciplinary backgrounds who have shaped technology to address their scholarly investigations. This book responds to the need for a coherent and focused analysis of the impact of discipline on the emergence of digital literary studies. I hope that this approach leaves the way open for others to think through digital practices in related areas such as game studies, new media studies, postcolonial studies, history, architecture, information studies, computer science, language studies, and archaeology.

I limit this study to the American academy, though I am fully aware that digital humanities in America did not develop in a vacuum. Professional organizations cross national boundaries, scholars move to jobs in different countries, and ideas are shared internationally. Yet formulations of digital work are constructed by national contexts shaped, in part, by funding and reward systems. Many digital projects in the United States, for example, have been supported by grants from the National Endowment for the Humanities (NEH) Start Up program. Focused on technological innovation, NEH Start Up grants have spurred the production of interoperable digital tools and technological standards. In other countries, such as Canada, larger digital research budgets and larger grant payouts have encouraged the pursuit of broader projects with huge collaborative teams. Additionally, reward systems have impacted the types of projects that scholars are willing to pursue. In countries where grant monies are necessary to secure tenure and promotion, digital humanities tends to be more prominent than in countries where grant funding is not valued. Digital projects that emphasize outreach and public impact are increasingly the norm in places like the United Kingdom, where funding models are driven by measurements that emphasize such criteria. Given the influence of the localized academic environment on the formation of digital humanities, it is pertinent to examine the practice within a particularized context.

In addition to situating digital humanities in its appropriate academic and national context, this project seeks to locate disciplinary influences on the construction of digital humanities. There is no doubt that the broader term digital humanities encompasses multiple areas of scholarly inquiry—from literary studies, to linguistics, to classics, to history and more—but the reality of the situation is that the institution that fuels scholarship—the academy—has not made much progress away from traditional disciplinary structures. The impact of interdisciplinary groups, departments, and scholarship is growing, but most scholars continue to be trained and practice in a disciplinary manner. *Traces of the Old, Uses of the New: The Emergence of Digital Literary Studies* grapples with these crucial issues by tracing the historical development, theoretical roots, and emergent trends of what is now being called digital humanities within literary studies. Conflicts within the larger digital humanities are revealed to be driven by long-held disciplinary understandings of approaches, methodologies, and values. Fields "do" scholarship differently. Digital humanities scholars have long operated under the false conception that new technological approaches and collaborative research negate the particularities of disciplinary training. This project seeks to expose the naturalized assumptions of interdisciplinarity in digital humanities.

A number of early published volumes discuss digital humanities, such as the *Blackwell Companion to Digital Humanities, Black-*

well Companion to Digital Literary Studies, Willard McCarty's *Humanities Computing*, and Jerome McGann's *Radiant Textuality: Literature after the World Wide Web*.[8] In such a rapidly changing area of inquiry, these works, which have served us well, are becoming dated. Luckily we are seeing an explosion of volumes focused on defining digital humanities, including *Understanding Digital Humanities*, edited by David M. Berry; Steven E. Jones's *The Emergence of Digital Humanities*; *Literary Studies in the Digital Age: An Evolving Anthology*, edited by Kenneth M. Price and Ray Siemens; *Digital Humanities*, edited by Anne Burdick et al.; *Defining Digital Humanities: A Reader*, edited by Melissa Terras et al., among others.[9] Some digital humanities volumes have focused on specific issues related to digital humanities, as do Susan Hockey's *Electronic Texts in the Humanities: Principles and Practice*; *Electronic Textual Editing*, edited by Lou Burnard, Katherine O'Brien O'Keeffe, and John Unsworth; and Dan Cohen's *Hacking the Academy*; conflicts within the field, such as *Debates in the Digital Humanities*, edited by Matthew K. Gold; or specific techniques of analysis, such as Matthew L. Jockers's *Macroanalysis: Digital Methods and Literary History*.[10] Perhaps unique in digital humanities is that print scholarship is beginning to wield less power in shaping the area as blog posts, tweets, listserv discussions, and digital projects gain attention. Alan Liu's influential post "Where Is Cultural Criticism in the Digital Humanities?," John Unsworth's early "What Is Humanities Computing and What Is Not?," Matthew Kirschenbaum's "What Is Digital Humanities and What's It Doing in English Departments?," or Bethany Nowviskie's illuminating "Eternal September of the Digital Humanities" have all made crucial interventions in digital humanities.[11] As the digital humanities writ large is shaped by a growing body of criticism, the exploration of specialized inquiry areas gains momentum. In addition to the above essays, full-length volumes including Daniel Cohen and Roy Rosenzweig's *Digital History: A Guide to Gathering, Preserving, and Presenting the Past on the Web* and my coedited volume *The American Literature Scholar in the Digital Age* become a necessary means of contouring our understanding of a dynamic area of scholarly inquiry.

Traces of the Old, Uses of the New: The Emergence of Digital Literary Studies analyzes the emergence of digital literary scholarship over the last 25 years. This project uses the scholarship and products of the digital turn to define historical and emergent trends; I analyze a range of materials including digital editions, digital archives, etexts, scholarly writing, digital artifacts (including tools and metadata), and interviews with key players in the field. While some critics have argued that digital humanities are an outlier to literary studies, this project reveals that many of the theoretical elements of literary studies are retained in digital literary studies. My project defines and analyzes four dominant areas of work in what I call digital literary studies: the digital edition form, the digital archive form, cultural studies approaches, and literary data approaches. I define each of these areas as foundational for digital literary studies and argue that these forms function within a continuum of production, with new techniques, such as datamining, gaining prestige within the field while never fully eliding earlier practice, such as the digital edition.

In chapter 1 I trace the foundational form of digital literary production, the digital edition. "The Rationale of Holism: Textual Studies, the Edition, and the Legacy of the Text Entire" argues that the centrality of the digital edition form that emerged from the combative field of textual studies transferred key ideas regarding texts and materiality to digital literary studies. Key concepts examined in the chapter include a distrust of the digital environment, the holistic text, and the desire for editorial control of the text. While textual studies has given digital literary studies an infrastructure through which we might represent the material text, our textual studies roots have also transferred the unfortunate legacy of the unfair representation of editing as uncritical and mechanical. Further, the editorial emphasis on purity and the inherited problematic treatment of issues of diversity has impacted the way in which digital literary studies has selected materials to digitize. Textual studies work has not neatly transferred into the digital nor has textual studies remained the dominant mode within digital literary studies, but the impact of textual studies on the field is undeniable.

Chapter 2, "The Era of the Archive: The New Historicist Movement and Digital Literary Studies," tracks the archive fever that overtook digital humanities in the 1990s, arguing that the digital archive was a contradictory form that sought to create an idealized archive. Work by Jerome McGann, Kenneth M. Price, Alan Liu, Martha Nell Smith, and others is examined to determine how specific tenets of new historicism, such as the use of an anecdote within a complex social system, form the digital archive model. Using examples from digital archives and print scholarship, I argue that the digital archive imagines the text within an expansive yet holistic system, with the textual materials designed to interact with a wide range of cultural materials. Tracking the rise of open access, web delivered archives, the chapter reveals the self-reflexivity of archive construction with particular attention to TEI/XML encoding approaches. Examination of theorists including Clifford Geertz, Jacques Derrida, and Michel Foucault exposes the impact of new historicist thinking on digital literary studies treatment of power structures, canon, and apparatus. The archival turn in American digital literary work has created a theoretical foundation for digital literary studies and allowed for the development of standardized approaches. I end the chapter by examining the growing tension between digital literature and digital history over the treatment of archives and argue that this tension is a prime example of the difficulty scholars have in defining the umbrella term of digital humanities.

Chapters 3 and 4 highlight emergent trends in digital literary production. Chapter 3, "What's In and What's Out?: Digital Canon Cautions," charts the impact of cultural studies approaches on digital humanities. Examining what I call digital recovery projects, the chapter focuses on activist, small-scale projects that used digitization to expand what such scholars saw as an outmoded new critical literary canon that excluded work by women, people of color, queers, and others. Embedded within contemporary understandings of the Internet, projects utilized entry-level technology skills to produce digital archives and curated, hyperlinked sites to digitize texts that would expand the canon. Cocurrent with individual scholarly production was the heyday of etext centers, focused on producing a large volume of digitized cultural materials. Examining early digital recovery projects including Alan Liu's *Voice of the Shuttle*, Jean Lee Cole's *The Winnifred Eaton Digital Archive*, the *Women Writers Project*, Glynis Carr's *The Online Archive of Nineteenth-Century U.S. Women's Writing*, and others, the chapter uncovers that not only has the early wave of small recovery projects slowed but projects have begun to disappear. I interrogate the impact of infrastructure, community, technological standards, and economics on the construction of digital literary canons, providing a roadmap for the construction of a broader digital literary canon.

Chapter 4, "Data and the Fragmented Text: Tools, Visualization, and Datamining or is Bigger Better?," focuses on tool development, visualization, and datamining, three crucial subareas of the interpretive bent of digital studies. Current work on visualizing and datamining is examined in the chapter, with careful attention to optical character recognition (OCR) and data sets. The chapter argues that there is an unresolved and longstanding division between interpretive and representational uses of technology within digital literary studies, particularly in the development of tools. Scholars interested in constructing tools to support digital work recognize that tool development is expensive and difficult and often leads to highly idiosyncratic, nonextensible, and unsustainable tools. The alternative, generalized tools, raises questions of use value, as many tools are not designed to address humanities concerns. Examining a variety of tools, such as Wordseer, Juxta, and the Versioning Machine, and datamining projects, such as Lauren Klein's work on James Hemings and Matthew Wilkens's analysis of Civil War American fiction, I argue that while such approaches are in their infancy, the possibilities are myriad. Instead of rejecting algorithmic approaches as flawed, we must focus on the construction of data in tandem with experimental algorithmic manipulations.

In the book's final chapter, "Notes on the Future of Digital Literary Studies," I consider the ways in which digital literary studies might come to terms with its history. Rejecting the hackneyed "what are the digital humanities" genre, the chapter revisits each of the formative fields discussed in the book to speculate how we might address current conflicts within the field. The chapter examines the current contours of debate in digital literary studies, with particular attention to formations of inside/outsider and resistance to the field by traditional literary scholars. With attention to current flash points of digital literary studies including the hack/yack divide, concerns regarding inclusivity, and the so-called innate conservatism of digital humanities, the chapter calls for a return to activist digital innovation that is divergent, not convergent.

It is crucial that scholars map the field of digital literary studies. My analysis of the development of digital literary studies itself owes much to new historicism, which theorizes that movements should be contextualized within power structures and examines the impact of theoretical, economic, social, and historical impacts on scholarship. By examining the evolution of what we have come to call digital literary studies within such contexts, we might better understand how the form has both shifted and maintained certain conceptions of text, literature, and scholarship. It is my hope that this volume will encourage interest in the emergence of digital scholarship and that others will choose to map technology applications within their area of expertise.

CHAPTER I

The Rationale of Holism

Textual Studies, the Edition, and the
Legacy of the Text Entire

For two millennia, the principal storage mechanism for the world's intellectual memory took the form of manuscript and printed books. These days, students and scholars have available to them a rapidly growing influx of digitized material, and the internet offers enormous possibilities for increasing the use of scanned older materials by making them more broadly available than would ever have been possible in a print environment. But we cannot provide posterity with an electronic copy of Walt Whitman's *Leaves of Grass* and, by so doing, absolve ourselves of the responsibility for preserving copies of the original, early, printed editions of Whitman's book and the manuscripts that lie behind them. *We have no right to deprive the future of the past.*

—Pamphlet, Rare Book School, the University of
    Virginia, 2009

Digital editions are some of the most visible early digital projects in digital literary studies, so predominant that one might argue that the digital edition is the primary form of the first generation of the field. For the purposes of this study, digital editions are those projects that meet the MLA "Guidelines for Editors of Scholarly Editions," and, as such, present a reliable text established by accuracy, adequacy, appropriateness, consistency, and explicitness.[1] Emerging from textual studies,[2] such "work explores the ideological structures and material processes that shape the transmission, reception, production, and interpretation of texts."[3] By probing the combative field of American textual studies in the 1990s, this chapter will reveal the roots of practices that are now accepted as standard in digital literary studies, such as the focus on digital editing and widely accepted models of form and layout of digital materials. These representations emerged out of what I call a "whole text" approach, a cohesive print-to-digital model that features interrelated textual materials, often in print book form, rather than an expansive and fragmented representation of text, as is increasingly the case with data-based deformations. The digital edition privileges the structure of the book, which is viewed as a self-contained entity with a naturalized means of displaying knowledge and is replicated in most aspects of digital edition creation, from display to the treatment of data. The replication of print in a digital form is designed to increase access to materials and aid examination of aspects of the original (illustrations, typography, etc.) that is rarely possible in modern reprints. While there is no doubt that such materials are beneficial to scholars, the early period of digital editions did not provide proof for the claim that digitization allows scholars to ask and answer questions in new ways, one crucial argument for the support of digital literary studies. In addition to this limitation, our textual studies roots brought the unfortunate marginalized status of editing to the greater digital literary studies, reinforcing an outsider position for our work that scholars continue to battle, and reinforcement of a traditional canon.

It is not an accident that textual studies scholars were intrigued with the digital in the early 1990s. Literary editorial scholarship was in upheaval.[4] Conflict within—authorial intent versus the social construction of the text—and without—the devaluation of editorial work by the larger discipline—made the field extremely unstable. As editors began to search for a way to create a better edition and to reinsert editing into the core of literary studies, they began to consider digital technologies as a possible help-mate.[5] This chapter is not intended to serve as a history of scholarly editing but to reveal how the history of scholarly editing has impacted the way that digital literary studies represents texts and to demonstrate that the conflict within textual studies approaches has, in some ways, seeded contemporary tensions regarding digital texts.

1951 marked the beginnings of the rationale papers, the essays that textual scholars wrote to advocate varying practices in the field. The 1951 "Rationale of Copy-Text" by W. W. Greg launched what came to be known as the Greg-Bowers model, "the dominant mode of Anglo-American textual criticism, institutionally and academically" and which dominated the field until challenged in the 1980s.[6] Greetham describes this school as "the copy-text school of eclectic editing designed to produce a reading clear-text whose features were a fulfillment of authorial intentions by the selection of authorially sanctioned substantive variants from different states of texts, and whose copy-text was selected on the basis of its accidentals being as close as possible to authorial usage."[7] The emphasis on the idealized and preexisting authorially sanctioned texts, the "Work," to use Tanselle's term, was premised on the belief that "[t]hose texts, being reports of works, must always be suspect; and, no matter how many of them we have, we never have enough information to know with certainty what the works consist of."[8] This approach situates textual studies as separate, "anterior to literary criticism," and "the scholar's first job" according to the first edition of *An Introduction to Bibliographical and Textual Studies*.[9] G. Thomas Tanselle took up the mantle of defending this version of textual studies, arguing that

the textual way of thinking—adjudicates between the com-
peting claims of a basic dilemma: the feeling, on the one
hand, that all artifacts, by their survival, deserve our respect,
either because they put us in touch with what has gone before or because we feel a social obligation to pass along in-
tact what we have received; and, on the other, the realization
that they may fail to represent, for a variety of reasons, what
their producers intended or what we feel we need, and that
without correction or repair they may be misleading guides
to the past, and without innovative change they may seem
unsatisfying.[10]

To Tanselle, "Such editing sought to establish a fixed, definitive
text, usually theorized as an ur-text marred by subsequent corruption in transmission."[11] The concern regarding the displacement of work within the editing process would figure predomi-
nantly in concerns about digital reproductions of literature, most
often a fear of loss of editorial control that will be discussed later
in this chapter.

Those scholars invested in Greg-Bowers editorial practices would also feel threatened by the displacement of editing
within the American academy. While textual studies work was
considered a central aspect of literary studies during the early
to mid-century, by the 1990s deconstruction and high literary
criticism had driven textual studies to the borders of the field.
Post-structuralists rejected the materiality of the text that those
invested in editorial work relished, broadening the concept of
text to a definition far more amorphous than that embraced by
those in the Greg-Bowers camp. Theorists such as Derrida refused the physical constraints attached to text, arguing for "a
'text' that is henceforth no longer a finished corpus of writing,
some content enclosed in a book or its margins, but a differential
network, a fabric of traces referring endlessly to something other
than itself, to other differential traces."[12] In response to Harold

Bloom's similarly stated comment that "there are *no* texts . . . but only interpretations," Thomas Tanselle responded, "he is obviously equating 'texts' with 'works' and asserting that works have no meanings independent of the interpretations of those who encounter them."[13] Such statements as those made by Bloom and Derrida attacked core values of those who embraced the Greg-Bowers editorial approach, with Tanselle noting:

> In recent years there has been an increasing tendency for literary critics to refer to literary works as "texts." In consequence, the term "textual criticism" has become ambiguous, some people regarding it as a synonym for "literary criticism." Traditionally, of course, "textual criticism" has meant the scholarly activity of studying the textual histories of verbal works in an effort to propose reliable texts of those works (according to one or another definition of correctness).[14]

Articles published in textual studies journals, "Textual and Literary Theory: Redrawing the Matrix" by D.C. Greetham, "Textual Criticism and Deconstruction" by G. Thomas Tanselle, and "Text as Matter, Concept, and Action" by Peter L. Shillingsburg, highlight the conflict. In Greetham's words, textual scholars took "on post-structuralists in a direct struggle for the body of the text."[15] The tension between criticism and textual studies has not dissolved and the legacy of that tension had a lasting impact on the development of digital humanities within the American academy.

The centrality of the digital edition form has intimately connected digital literary studies to traditional textual studies approaches in the minds of many critics, in turn replicating splits between textual studies and literary criticism. The rejection of textual studies by literary criticism has been discussed in great detail within textual studies, but there has been little consideration of the duplication of such splits within digital humanities *because of* the roots of textual studies. In part, the rejection of digital literary studies has occurred because of the legacy of associating edition building with mechanical, applied work, leading to the charge of uncomplicated, simplistic, and mechanistic digital literary studies work. Michael Groden sums up the original textual studies/literary criticism divide: "Literary theorists and critics have tended to see editing and bibliography as activities that are preliminary to criticism and the textual theorists and critics themselves as concerned only with empirical evidence, often with minute details (commas, watermarks)."[16] In his notorious "The Fruits of the MLA," Edmund Wilson argues that textual editors have monopolized and suppressed the pleasure of literature and dampened the impact of literature across the wider culture.[17] The charge of overt technicality and devotion to minutia at the exclusion of literary pleasure is similar to critiques of digital editing. In Ian Small's understanding of a digital editor, "he or she must cease to edit, in the sense of exercising any form of control or judgment. The postmodernist hypertext editor apparently needs only to supply data; he or she need not order it." Small continues by representing the editor as powerless: "In the process, though, that editor appears also to have been stripped of any effective agency, authority, or responsibility . . . The logic of such a move would be to de-skill and demote the very individuals, text-editors and text-theorists, whose interests it is supposed to promote."[18] The charges against digital editing are long standing, nearly engrained in contemporary critical approaches, which views editing, whether print or digital, as a return to conservative critical approaches to literature. Leroy F. Searle points out that "[f]or an earlier generation, the vocation of editorial scholarship often seemed a haven (if not the very citadel) of intellectual probity, in which one could practice a science—mild and respectful, if sometimes dull—without being drawn into the relatively unregulated life of literary criticism and theory, where, as I.A. Richards remarked after a lifetime of experience with it, 'an indecent disregard of fact is still current form.'"[19] The argument voiced by Searle is part of a contiguous arc, where the history of textual studies work has strongly influenced the way in which digital humanities has become understood.

Further, the displacement of editing and the impact on digital humanities has happened within a particularized national context that has adversely impacted American work in digital editing. Scholars including Hans Gabler, G. Thomas Tanselle, and Jerome McGann[20] are quick to point out that the treatment and trajectory of the field differs greatly by nationality. Robert Hume, in "The Aims and Uses of 'Textual Studies,'" notes that textual studies has reached a ". . . low standing . . . in North American English departments . . . Few major institutions emphasize editing or bibliographic scholarship, and bright students are rarely encouraged to take up these lines of work. The bibliography/literary criticism dichotomy has become a chasm over the last twenty or thirty years, with critics increasingly neglectful and even contemptuous of bibliographic scholarship."[21] The lack of standing in North American departments, where textual studies work is often considered "just editing" by those invested in literary criticism, is not so in the European academy where textual studies continues to hold an important position within academia. Perhaps this is because, as Hume notes, Anglo-American editing is distinctly different than European editing, where "literary editing has rarely been carried out with much respect for the Greg-Bowers program."[22] Hans Gabler likewise points to the "dichotomy between criticism and scholarship," which he argues is "an American division . . . in the first place; responsible, I believe for much in the present modern topography of the academic landscape in English, American, and modern languages and literatures; and never whole-heartedly embraced as a mode of self-definition in literary studies in Europe."[23] The digital turn has done little to bring European and American attitudes toward textual studies work together. Europeans have produced a far greater number of digital editions and the form continues to have a great deal of currency. Though digital editions are currently produced in the United States, the position of editing within the American academy has meant that those working on such projects continue to find their work stigmatized.

However, the impact of editorial displacement from the mainstream American academy is not equally distributed. The dominance of the Greg-Bowers approach was contested by those who championed a reevaluation of the theoretical framework of textual studies, such as Jerome McGann, D. F. McKenzie, and David Greetham. McGann took on the Greg-Bowers school's approach to editing in the early 1980s after his experience with editing Byron. In his 1983 *Critique of Modern Textual Criticism*, McGann challenged those that privileged the position of author in the text, arguing that such ideas "so emphasize the autonomy of the isolated author as to distort our theoretical grasp of the 'mode of existence of a literary work of art' (a mode of existence which is fundamentally social rather than personal)."[24] Designed to represent a production process rather than individual moment of creation, the social text criticism proposed by McGann is described by Greetham as "an alternative view of composition, in which the entire history of the work is a fit subject for textual scholarship, and even posthumous changes by editors, publishers, friends and relations, are to be considered a perfectly valid part of the text read as a social construct."[25] McGann's challenge to the Greg-Bowers approach generated not only a great deal of tension within the field but would lay the groundwork for the move from digital edition to digital archive that will be discussed in the next chapter.

During the height of digital editing, editors invested in producing high quality scholarly editions were increasingly concerned about the future of edition production. Regardless of how the scholar viewed his or her school of editing, limitations of print technologies and the economics of scholarly publication increasingly constrained textual and bibliographical scholarship. Peter Shillingsburg provides a useful analysis of issues of length, completeness, and the economics of scholarly publication in a 1996 article:

> A scholarly edition is a thick book (five hundred to a thousand pages) printed on acid-free paper guaranteed for 350 years, in sturdy bindings, with a list of ten to twenty editors and advisory editors, published by a reputable academic press and costing a minimum of fifty dollars, but more often over one hundred. It contains a Pure Virgin Text or, unironically, a Fully Restored one. Already a thick tome because of the historical and textual introductions and textual apparatus, scholarly editions frequently exclude explanatory annotations because the space they require would add unduly to the cost (already out of the reach of ordinary mortals and nearly out of reach for the ordinary research library).[26]

Print, as Shillingsburg and many other critics have pointed out, is very stable. It is a known form, has a workflow for production, and survives over a fairly long time period. While acknowledging that print is superior in many ways, textual studies scholars recognized that the form was plagued with worrying restrictions. Scholarly editions are expensive to publish and page numbers are limited.[27] The annotations and apparatus are often restricted or excluded, driven by economic and print size concerns that lead to the production of an unsatisfactory scholarly product. Even more alarming since the publication of Shillingsburg's article, the scholarly publishing field has contracted almost to the point of nonexistence. The MLA Ad Hoc Committee on Scholarly Publishing presented sobering findings in their 2002 report,[28] noting that declining subsidies of university presses and decreases for library acquisitions has caused a substantial drop in sales while the numbers of faculty who are required to produce a monograph publication for tenure and promotion has increased, putting undue pressure on the already fragile system. Scholarly editions, in particular, stated the committee, are under threat because of cost, time of production, and NEH funding cuts.[29] Such constrictions drove those interested in producing editions to consider experimental forms of the digital edition.

Imagining how the digital environment would best serve textual studies consumed scholars in the 1990s. Even the most traditional textual studies scholars recognized that they needed to confront the digital, whether to embrace, to alter, or to reject the new technology. Richard Finneran would call the digital a "fundamental paradigm shift,"[30] and David Greetham, who imagined "the fully open, *scriptable*, postmodernist edition of literature," argued that we "will need the facilities of electronic, reader-driven editions to achieve the flexibility and lack of closure that *differance* observes."[31] Still other scholars, such as Peter Shillingsburg and Jerome McGann, developed digital tools and editions and argued for the centrality of digital work to textual studies. Even G. Thomas Tanselle recognized that the digital was useful to editorial work, though he posited a far more constrained view of the power of technology: "Computerization is simply the latest chapter in the long story of facilitating the reproduction and alteration of texts; what remains constant is the inseparability of recorded language from the technology that produced it and makes it accessible."[32] While these scholars didn't agree about *how* the digital should be applied to textual studies work, they all acknowledged that the digital *would* impact scholarship.

During this period, groundbreaking scholarship would produce a textual studies core within digital literary studies. From Peter Shillingsburg's early *Scholarly Editing in the Computer Age* to Jerome McGann's later *Radiant Textuality*, many textual studies scholars professed their investment in technology and the text. Collections, including *The Literary Text in the Digital Age* and *Electronic Textual Editing*, helped to define digital humanities with a particularized textual studies slant.[33] The very same tensions that caused scholarly battles among editors of print editions would emerge in the creation of digital editions, a legacy that remains with us today. As scholars began to imagine how the digital might help them build a better edition, they also were forced to engage, once again, in the very debates that split textual studies practice. What, exactly, is a text? What is the role of the editor? How does one understand an individual item in relation to many items? For a portion of American textual studies scholars, primarily those committed to the Greg-Bowers school, digital editions emphasized a continued integrity of the object of study. Experimental digital editions including *The Electronic Beowulf*, *The Canterbury Tales Project*, and *The Piers Plowman Project*[34] adopted tool-based technology approaches to enact best practices in the new environment and launched digital editing that focused on what the MLA Committee on Scholarly Editions described as "the scholarly edition's basic task"—"to present a reliable text."[35] Concerns about reliability in the new digital environment were central to presentations of texts, with Peter Shillingsburg sounding the alarm over poor quality texts found in online sources like Project Gutenberg and about an overreliance on computers, which Shillingsburg describes as "just a convenience."[36] This early treatment of tools as a means to the end, tools as applications to manipulate the text into a representative form, would remain one important legacy of textual studies.

Perhaps the greatest impact of the textual studies tradition is the emphasis on a whole text approach, a digital edition that is not deformed and a trustworthy text that has been subjected to editorial control. Peter Shillingsburg has very vocally argued for a holistic approach to text, "a recognition of the textual condition understood whole," and perhaps his words have become more strident in recent years as datamining and visualization proponents have pushed for a destabilized or even fragmented text.[37]

In *Scholarly Editing in the Computer Age*, Shillingsburg restates "editing is, above all else, a matter of forms." The "forms, the details of presentation, are often thought to be the responsibility of editors."[38] Accordingly, tools, whether the computer, interface, database, or collation program, were designed to produce editions that emphasized continuity of form and a clear recognition of materiality. The centrality of form that Shillingsburg points to has transferred into digital literary studies and is apparent in the way in which interface represents the physical object. For many early edition projects, the digital interface mimics the traditional book structure and includes core elements of the book such as the table of contents, page display, and index. For example, when *Studies in Bibliography* (*SB*) was brought online by the University of Virginia Electronic Text (Etext) Center in 1995 it maintained the centrality of the book through the interface (see fig. 1.1).

Form, in such editions, was a correlation to materiality, not a means of manipulation. In his foreword to *Electronic Textual Editing*, Tanselle[39] accepts that the digital is a useful medium in which to publish the edition, but warns that "when the excitement leads to the idea that the computer alters the ontology of texts and makes possible new kinds of reading and analysis, it has gone too far."[40] The binary that Tanselle sets up—digital as a tool versus the digital as a means to new forms, ontologies, reading, or analysis—is a theme replicated across digital textual scholarship and projects. Or, as Speed Hill has written, "I can live with technological change per se, but I fear the more fundamental shift in the aims and purposes of scholarly editing that threatens the work we invest in preserving the artifacts we cherish. Technological change overvalues the new, the computer-hip, the gee-whiz factor, while devaluing editions that appear in the form and format of the traditional code."[41] David Gants also sees the digital environment as a way to represent "a well-designed electronic edition" that "can exploit the flexibility of the digital medium and avoid the need to deform the text; it can shift and adapt to the

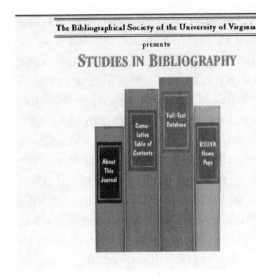

Fig. 1.1. Image from entry page, *Studies in Bibliography* website, circa 2000. (Bibliographical Society of Virginia, Etext Center, the University of Virginia. http://etext.virginia. edu/bsuva/sb.)

needs of the individual user, encouraging us, as Tanselle notes, to become collaborators."[42] In each of these understandings of digital editing the end goal remains the same—"to avoid the need to deform the text." Even those who are some of the staunchest supporters of digital innovation recognize that early digital edition work did little more than replicate the print structure. Peter Robinson, for example, acknowledges the imitative qualities of early digital textual studies projects: "The first missing aspect is that up to now, almost without exception, no scholarly electronic edition has presented material which could not have been presented in book form, nor indeed presented this material in a manner significantly different from that which could have been managed in print."[43] It is the "sameness" of digital that is the reassuring thread that runs through early digital work, and the hallmark of the early digital edition is the stability, the reassurance, of a form that replicates print.

While the form remained stable, scholars hoped that technology would allow editors to create digital versions that would be "better than" print editions. Rejecting what some saw as the textual instability advocated by social text theorists like Jerome McGann, digital editors tried to create a digital replica, a work in much the sense of Tanselle. States Shillingsburg, "In the 'work represented' I argue that just as a researcher in a library requesting the first edition of a work would reject a transcription of that edition as a basis for research, so a researcher using an electronic edition should also reject a transcript. An image is, after all, as close as one can get, electronically, to the original. The transcript becomes a convenience for searching, while the original (or a good image of it) continues to be used as the real thing."[44] Hill echoes this critique in his response to McGann's digital work, which he says embraces "a device designed for and dedicated to the de-materialization—for that's what the term 'digitization' really means—of that very same material artifact into a signal stream made up of zillions of offs and ons, wholly dependent on a complex infrastructure over which none of us has any control."[45] The centrality of the material object would loom large in early digital edition development, as editors battled to assert control over the textual representation.

The *Electronic Beowulf* (1994) is an exemplar of the work made stable within the digital environment. Rife with textual studies apparatus, *Beowulf* includes multiple manuscripts, transcriptions, definitions and other types of support materials, and illustrations from the one original manuscript that "far exceed the appearance of any published black-and-white facsimiles," effectively becoming a value added facsimile edition, an idealized edition that is broader and more complete than any previous print edition.[46] The "better than print" edition allows scholars to thumb through the fragile pages of the physical manuscripts, gathered together in their entirety rather than spread throughout numerous libraries around the world, and to use technology to collate the various transcriptions. Further, the digital edition contains "hundreds of fiber-optic readings of hidden letters and ultraviolet readings of erased text from the early 11th-century manuscript" and "read-

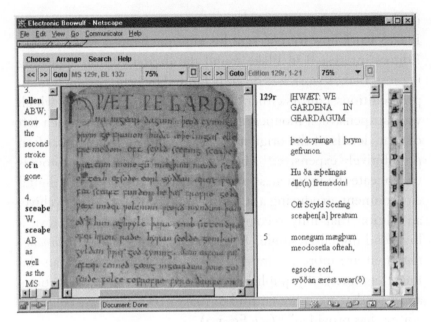

Fig. 1.2. A manuscript image and transcription from the *Electronic Beowulf* CD-ROM. (From William Kilbride, reviewer. "Whose Beowulf is it anyway? Review of *Electronic Beowulf* [CD-Rom]." *Internet Archaeology* 9, 2000. http://dx.doi.org/10.11141/ia.9.12.)

ings that were visible to J. J. Conybeare in 1817, before the 19th-century binding frames covered the burnt edges of the manuscript; and selections from other documents needed to restore the damaged text"[47] (see fig. 1.2).

The ability to utilize computer techniques to find hidden letters, erasures, and to reinstate lost sections of the text encapsulates the age of the digital edition where technology was used "to draw attention back to the manuscript."[48] Further, the *Beowulf* edition enforces the idea of the work, where the restored text is as close to the idealized original as possible. Technology, in the age of the digital edition, is useful because it allows the editor to publish the material text as it was believed to be originally constructed.

Joe Viscomi, an editor of *The William Blake Archive*, likewise sees the digital environment as a way to resolve problems found in the production of a traditional print edition, in the case of Blake's work how to represent his multiple hand-colored poems. Editors interested in Blake found the digital edition appealing because Blake's work was severely limited by print production. In print editions, editors either developed a text only edition, which was inexpensive, a monochromatic reproduction, and which left out the details of the original, or hand-colored collotypes, often prohibitively expensive.[49] The *Blake Archive* developed protocols to replicate the uniqueness of the individual images in the digital environment, producing a stunning and groundbreaking archive, an edition that fully recognizes the individual material text, a high-end digital facsimile. The *Blake Archive* supplies *"reproductions* that are more accurate in color, detail, and scale than the finest commercially published photomechanical reproductions and *texts* that are more faithful to Blake's own than any collected edition has provided"[50] (see fig. 1.3).

The project was awarded the 2003 MLA Prize for a Distinguished Scholarly Edition, an honor rightly bestowed on the edition for its use of the digital to make a better edition, one of the most fully realized representations of the textual studies tradition brought digital. Yet I want to emphasize that the *Blake Archive*'s success depends in large part on its recognizable form that bridges the gap between traditional textual studies work and digital humanities. The *Blake Archive*'s insistence on the centrality of image to the digital edition speaks to the continued distrust of technological interpretations of the original work. The editors note, "our images are not intended to be 'archival' in the sense sometimes intended—virtual copies that might stand in for originals after a fire," even while they make every attempt to reproduce the physical object, from scale to resolution to color suggesting that the editors continue to view the material object as unique and, ultimately, unreproducable.[51] The tension between the physical object and how it is represented, the ultimate distrust of the technological representation would be a hallmark

Fig. 1.3. Image from *Songs of Innocence and of Experience, The William Blake Archive.* http://www.blakearchive.org/exist/blake/archive/object.xq?objectid=songsie.z.illbk.20&java=no.

of the digital edition. Philip Cohen is one of many editors who were concerned about the increasing ability of anyone to edit and produce a text, of digital programs that "allow readers to create different combinations of the extant texts." To Cohen, and other editors, electronic approaches will not mean "the end of textual scholarship because assembling electronic editions and accounting for textual variations will still require print."[52] Editors hoped that the digital environment would allow for improved editing, but they resisted what they feared would lead to a deformation of the text and the possibility of unschooled editorial intervention.

Another way to fix the text and to assure quality within the digital environment was to partner with scholarly presses. During this period the University of Michigan produced *Piers Plowman*; the University of Kentucky, in partnership with the British Library, produced the *Electronic Beowulf*; the University of Virginia produced the presidential papers, including the Adams and Thomas Jefferson Papers, and a variety of nineteenth-century literary editions, such as *Clotel* by William Wells Brown and Herman Melville's *Typee*; and Cambridge University Press published portions of the *Canterbury Tales Project*. New organizations were formed to ensure the quality of digital publications. SEENET, the Society for Early English & Norse Electronic Texts, publisher of *Caedmon's Hymn, Piers Plowman*, and other digital editions, "was established in the 1990s to gain the benefits of new electronic technology without sacrificing what scholars have learned about textual criticism and its sister disciplines."[53] SEENET's digital editions were modeled on a "long-established book publication series, Medieval Academy Books (MAB), which is overseen by the Publications Advisory Board and published in collaboration with the University of Toronto Press. Like MAB, the SEENET series focuses on editions and scholarly tools of importance to medieval studies. And like MAB, the SEENET series is made possible by working in partnership with an established press."[54] SEENET utilized a production to distribution process that closely followed print production, a model common among scholarly publishers interested in going digital. The press would accept a scholar's work and then vet that work through their network of experts, assuring the quality of the edition. Once the project was accepted, the press would develop an infrastructure through which to publish the project. The user would purchase either a subscription to a web-based edition or a CD-ROM. The workflow was remarkably similar to that of a print edition, which maintained the various checks on quality and control over output, a means of assuaging fears of digital instability.[55] Concerned about textual production in an age where editorial control was eroding, editors reasserted their centrality by linking their work to the known marker of authenticity, the scholarly publishing house.

The imprimatur of the scholarly publishing house helped to validate the new digital form, but scholars remained committed to a physical version of their edition, the CD-ROM. The Compact Disc Read-Only Memory was a data disc that could be imprinted and locked, immune to manipulation by the user. Like a book, a CD could be published, distributed, and owned. It could be placed on a shelf, taken down and perused, then returned to the shelf to be enjoyed at a later date. Peter Robinson, who initially published his ambitious *Canterbury Tales* digital editions with a scholarly press, Cambridge, and later his own publishing company, Scholarly Digital Editions, argues that the publication methods in the early to mid-1990s made the CD-ROM the preferred form of publication as scholars believed it to be a far more stable technology than the web.[56] The CD-ROM allowed the publisher to replicate the print infrastructure for publishing, acquiring and lending, making it, according to Hockey, the "medium of choice for many electronic publications, largely because it is easier for publishers and librarians to handle. It fits in better with procedures for handling books and in some ways can be seen as an extension of them."[57] The CD, with its ability to be transported, to be bought and sold, with its ability to mimic the book's organizational structure was a reassuring form to those concerned about the decline of editorial control.

Other advances in digital literary scholarship, such as the TEI/XML, are in line with concerns about the stabilized, editorially controlled whole text. The TEI was established in 1987 by The Working Committee on Text Encoding Practices of the Association for Computers and Humanities and, over its almost forty years of development, has risen to become the de facto encoding approach for digital texts. The members of the initial TEI Working Committee[58] requested an NEH Emergency Grant to "develop and promote guidelines for standard text-encoding practices in preparing machine-readable texts for scholarly research."[59] The committee decided to modify SGML with "a set of markup tags, and to define how they can be used."[60] By 1990 the TEI Working Committee would publish its first guidelines, and in January of 1999, the TEI consortium was formed. The TEI is a useful tool and mastery of TEI markup is often considered to be a base skill for digital literary studies, but practitioners admit that it is problematic for certain types of editorial purposes. Numerous scholars have pointed to the limitations of the TEI for complex textual representations,[61] but an examination of the history and evolution of TEI suggests that the problem lies, to some degree, in the TEI's initial conception, as the TEI was not originally constructed for use by literary editors. The 1987 TEI NEH grant shows participation from linguists and literary scholars, but of those involved in the 1987 Working Committee not one of the originators of the TEI was a literary textual scholar. Lou Burnard and C. M. Sperberg-McQueen had backgrounds in English and comparative literature but worked within computing. David Barnard and Nancy Ide were in computer science departments. David Chesnutt was a historian and documentary editor working with historical papers. The specialized needs of edition building literary scholars, then, were not central to the goals of the original TEI working group. Further, at the historical moment when TEI was proposed, historical and literary editorial methodologies were divergent. Clashes between historians and literary editors were driven public by G. Thomas Tanselle, who delivered a blistering talk at the American Documentary Editing conference in the late 1980s condemning historical editing. Tanselle complained in his related 1986 article "Historicism and Critical Editing":

> Even though many historical editors have practiced critical editing in the sense that they have normalized or regularized certain features of their texts, and have not simply

produced diplomatic transcriptions, many of them have not been able to see the value of the further step that literary editors have often taken when dealing with multiple texts of a single work, the step of emending one text with variants from another. Not having progressed beyond this elementary stage in the process of thinking about editing, they have not been in a position to enter into the more sophisticated discussions of historicism in critical editing. It is an unfortunate fact that what historians have published on the subject of editing has not contributed to the development of editorial theory.[62]

The initial NEH grant notes that TEI will focus on the needs "of text-oriented historical research (including documentary editing) which are similar in nature"[63] and states that the consortium would invite participation from the American Documentary Editing group, a scholarly group that draws membership from historical and literary editors. While this statement seems inclusive, the grant qualifies its inclusion by stating that they would invite the American Historical Association and historical editors, not literary editors or members of the Modern Language Association. This strange elision suggests that at least some members of the TEI consortium were well aware of the tensions between historical and literary editing and, with this notation the TEI was initially attuned to historical editing at the exclusion of literary editing.[64] The exclusion of literary textual editing from the formative TEI grant implies that the type of markup initially imagined would be more useful to historical editing than literary editing. Therefore, it is not surprising that the TEI has been criticized by literary scholars interested in using the markup language. McGann states,

> TEI's emergence exposed the deep flaw in the TEI representation of texts. A text is not an Ordered Hierarchy of Content Objects; it is a manifold of an indeterminate

number of possible ordered hierarchies. Every text, every element of every text, is n-dimensional, depending on what you choose to regard as contextually relevant. This basic truth about representational media of all kinds, not just "texts", did not become so graphically apparent to scholars until the TEI consortium set out to implement its alternative conceptual design. The failure of the OHCO thesis proved to be the TEI's greatest contribution to textual and media studies, and to the further development of the TEI itself.[65]

TEI works well for marking the structure of the text, but representation of complicated editorial markings and variants that a scholar editing a literary manuscript might be interested in representing presents a much more difficult challenge. While those involved with the Poughkeepsie Principles, the initial stated goals of the TEI, were not outwardly hostile toward literary editing, the apparent differences in methodology cannot be overstated. The 1999 formation of the TEI consortium signaled the beginning of the TEI's desire to meet the needs of literary editorial scholars. With John Unsworth's leadership, the MLA was named a partner in the consortium, signaling a ground shift in the TEI's approach to literature. The consortium agreement emphasized that "[t]he key constituencies for the TEI, then, are the various scholarly communities involved in text encoding (linguists, historians, textual theorists, literary historians, etc.), and libraries . . ."[66] Though the TEI shifted course, the legacy of their initial methodology continues to produce certain well documented limitations for those interested in applying TEI markup to literary texts. For Peter Shillingsburg and other editors, a whole text solution to digital editing would be solved through alternative technological solutions. Concerned about "file security and avoiding the conflicts and corruptions endemic to Wiki solutions," editing of texts by the masses, Shillingsburg has repeatedly called for a stand-

off markup solution, where a text remains untouched and manipulation occurs outside of the pristine whole.[67] Shillingsburg,
like most digital editors of this period, is concerned that highly
trained editors and their skills are devalued in the new environment and, in response, he calls for "a tagging tool that will allow
textual scholars (not highly trained technical assistants) to associ-
ate their analytical tagging as stand-off mark-up to already existing texts." Such an approach will "allow others to add tagging
without affecting the files already on offer," protecting the text
from errors.[68] Standoff markup is a solution posed to protect the
editorially controlled text, a direct response to the potential for
manipulations of texts marked with TEI.

The digital edition has had a great impact on digital literary
studies and remains a central, visible form of digital literary production, so successful that Kenneth Price has stated that "digital
work has achieved primacy only for editions."[69] Current projects,
such as the *Melville Electronic Library*, continue to explore how
best to position the editor in relationship to technology.[70] For
Melville, and project director John Bryant, editing is a far more
interactive process than imagined by early digital edition creators, with technology a helpmate for collaboration. Following
Bryant's theory of fluid textuality, where texts are always evolving due to interventions from a myriad of participants, *Melville*
rejects a stabilization of one version of a text and makes visible
multiple versions and changes, recording each instance while allowing users to make and record their own interventions. Clearly
one legacy of the digital edition work is a continued evaluation
of the position of the editor and the text. The primacy of the
digital in edition production has also shifted the future of digital editions. Edition building is now most likely to occur in the
digital environment, driven by limitations of press support, expansive opportunities for image-based editions, and technological manipulation of materials. Even long-standing print editing
projects, from the Founding Father's documents to Shakespeare,

have turned to digital publication. On the other hand, digital edition practices were and are interwoven into digital literary studies, impacting the way that we understand current digital literary studies production.

As this chapter reveals, questions regarding scholarly intervention, the material object and digital surrogates, and the treatment of computer deformation of texts are all legacies of the digital edition form. Unfortunately the history and impact of digital editions is often overlooked or misunderstood by many digital humanities practitioners. Editions are recognized early digital forms, but textual studies approaches, from TEI to interface design, have become naturalized in the field without a clear understanding of their historical context. Further, some in the digital humanities community have begun to view digital edition building as technologically unsophisticated, in effect echoing Ian Small's view of editing as "a largely pragmatic, unsophisticated activity."[71] Financial support for digital editing is difficult to obtain and recognition of scholarly skill required for edition building remains low. On the other end of the spectrum, however, is the overreliance on the edition form, long a problem in textual studies. Jerome McGann warned of the dangers of such an approach in his predigital 1985 essay "The Monks and the Giants: Textual and Bibliographical Studies and the Interpretation of Literary Works":

> If textual and bibliographical studies are to have a significant impact on literary interpretation, textual criticism will have to be reconceptualized along lines that transcend an editorial theory. Of course, an editorial perspective on the principles of textual criticism is imperative under certain circumstances. Nevertheless, such a perspective only tends to obscure matters when the central issue is the relation of textual scholarship to literary meaning.[72]

McGann's warning continues to be appropriate. An overreliance on a particularized approach or methodology that excludes expansion or innovation is as dangerous as the lack of historical understanding of textual studies approaches. Perhaps Margaret Ezell has articulated this most concisely. In discussing the move to "e-editions," she notes, "it becomes clear to me that while we increasingly have the ability to digitalize any text we please— although there are certainly grounds for debate how well the digitalized images capture the features of the material original— editors do not please to select certain types of material and this is in part because perhaps we are not yet changing some of the basic assumptions about what an 'edition' does, or in Hunter's terms, what is 'appropriate.'"[73] We need to be mindful of, but not bound to, textual studies approaches revealing how the digital edition has transferred certain representations into naturalized digital literary practice.

Textual studies has a problematic relationship to diversity that has unfortunately transferred to current digital literary scholarship. Martha Nell Smith has pointed to the rigid and exclusive normative practices in textual studies and calls for editing to "take into account the 'messy' facts of authorship, production, and reception: race, class, gender, and sexuality."[74] Of her first attendance at the Society for Textual Studies (STS) conference, the major international society meeting for academic editors, she noticed that "[m]ore than a few participants in STS seemed to think of it as a space free from all the messiness of questions of identity and politics."[75] While editors may have seen themselves as forced out of the mainstream of academic literary studies, their resistance to issues of gender, race, class, and sexuality in large part made them outsiders to normative practice within the broader field. Julia Flanders has examined the early treatment of gender in editing and argues that "the error-ridden manuscript is figured in the rhetoric of the humanist scholar, as an unchaste female body which has suffered 'corruption' . . . as a result of sexual attack."[76] The editor, then, must restore "a lost wholeness" by "intervening in the text and altering it yet more so as to cover over the places of its corruption."[77] The figuration of the corrupt text is apparent in the Greg-Bowers approach to editing as well. Fredson Bowers, to many the grandfather of modern textual studies, was obsessively concerned about issues of textual purity. In *Textual Criticism and the Literary Critics* he writes, "the most important concern of the textual bibliographer is to guard the purity of the important basic documents of our literature and culture . . . One can no more permit 'just a little corruption' to pass unheeded in the transmission of our literary heritage than 'just a little sin' was possible in Eden."[78] Bowers' correlation between textual purity and Eve's original sin, the "little sin" that caused the fall from Eden, reveals just how deep-seated problematic representations of gender are to the formation of ideas regarding editing. In fact, Bowers' interest in purity has an odd correlation to his hobby, dog breeding. In his tribute to Bowers, "The Life and Work of Fredson Bowers," Tanselle points to Bower's interest in breed standards of the Irish Wolfhounds that he bred, showed, and eventually judged:

> That Bowers should have involved himself actively in this matter [breed standards] is not surprising, for his mind was attracted to categorization and systematization, and the problem was not unlike the bibliographical question he later addressed concerning the description of "ideal" copies of books, abstracted from the idiosyncrasies of actual surviving copies. In one of his most thoughtful columns on the wolfhound standard (January 1939), he wrote that "it is of the utmost importance that a clear and reasonably definite set of rules be laid down for judging any breed if the great benefit which dog shows confer upon improving the breed is not to turn into a boomerang by reason of such diverse judging that no practical ideal can be ascertained."[79]

Bowers interest in "rules" related to purity underpins the notion that editing has indeed been limited in scope and approach and is often exclusionary of particular texts. If the editor's goal is to protect the pure text, according to Bowers, then it should come as no surprise that textual studies scholars resisted calls to investigate issues of diversity. The messiness of such outside forces threatened to disrupt foundational ideas about editing. This history is part of digital editing, which likewise struggled with how to protect the text.

As this chapter suggests, the digital edition was the most prevalent form of the first generation of digital literary work in the United States. While textual studies work has not neatly transferred into digital literary studies nor has textual studies remained the dominant mode, the form is still useful and necessary, and there is no reason to believe that we won't continue to see digital editions produced under the auspices of digital humanities work. Digital humanists must not lose sight of the textual studies methodological and theoretical approaches that underpin the field. To do so is not only to negate important early work but to deny crucial scholarly projects needed to advance literary studies. At the same time, digital literary scholars must recognize how such forms impact the types of scholarly questions that we might ask, excavating the impact of textual studies methodology and theory.

CHAPTER 2

The Era of the Archive

*The New Historicist Movement and
Digital Literary Studies*

Out of the vast array of textual traces in a culture, the identi-
fication of units suitable for analysis is problematized. If every
trace of a culture is part of a massive text, how can one identify the boundaries of these units? What is the appropriate
scale? There are, we conclude, no abstract, purely theoretical answers to these questions. To a considerable extent the
units are given by the archive itself-that is, we almost always
receive works whose boundaries have already been defined
by the technology and generic assumptions of the original
makers and readers. But new historicism undertakes to call
these assumptions into question and treat them as part of the
history that needs to be interpreted.
—Catherine Gallagher and Stephen Greenblatt,
Practicing New Historicism, 14–15

I begin with one of "my own traveler's anecdotes" from a journey
to digital humanities.[1] In 1996, I attended the American Literature Association (ALA) meeting held in San Diego, California. I
was particularly interested in the "New Vistas in Whitman Studies" panel during which my former professor, Kenneth Price,
was to introduce his new scholarly project, something he called

The Walt Whitman Archive (*WWA*). The large group of attendees waited impatiently while the conference organizers struggled to set up a computer projector, probably the very first such technology used at ALA. As the talk began, murmurs were heard critiquing the technological issues that slowed the timely start of the presentation. Yet, as Price began to show page after page of Whitman's manuscripts, people in the room started to nod. Such was the era of the digital archive, where scholars outside of specialized fields of literary studies began to come into contact with digital humanities forms.

Digital edition production peaked in the early 1990s, and by the mid-1990s the digital archive began to emerge as the dominant form in American digital literary studies. The shift from edition to archive is not uniform, with digital edition production continuing into the contemporary period.[2] Instead, the digital archive became the dominant, but not exclusive, form in American digital literary studies. The shift from digital edition to digital archive is related, in large part, to the rise of new historicism. While only a handful of scholars working within the new historicist framework embraced digital scholarship, their incorporation of new historicist theories into technological methodology has defined the field. Jerome McGann, *The Rossetti Archive* (*RA*); Kenneth Price, *The Whitman Archive* (*WWA*); Martha Nell Smith, the *Dickinson Electronic Archives* (*DEA*); Cathy Davidson, HASTAC; Alan Liu, *Romantic Chronology*; and even Stephen Greenblatt, with his undergraduate course "A Silk Road Course: Travel and Transformation on the High Seas: An Imaginary Journey in the Early 17th Century," have experimented with digital technologies.[3] Students of these scholars—including Andrew Jewell, *The Willa Cather Archive*; Amanda Gailey, *Race and Children's Literature of the Gilded Age*; and Craig A. Warren, the *Ambrose Bierce Project*—have continued the trend. Jerome McGann's creation of NINES, the Networked Infrastructure for Nineteenth-Century Electronic Scholarship, coalesced the individual efforts of scholars and positioned the archive in the center of the digital literary field. As the digital archive moved to the center of digital literary studies, so too did new historicist thinking. Multiple versions of one text are not the centerpiece of the digital archive as they are in the digital edition; the text is understood to be in conversation with an ever-widening gyre of materials that include literary, cultural, and historical texts. This new historicist conception of the archive imagines the text within an expansive system, with the textual materials positioned in a network of conversation with a wide range of cultural materials. Scholars working within the rubric of new historicism positioned the physical archive and print materials as the centerpieces of their work. The digital environment would serve as a mechanism for refining the archive.

In 1982, Stephen Greenblatt used the term new historicism in his introduction to the *Genre* special issue, *The Power of Forms in the English Renaissance*. While there are other, earlier uses of the term, Greenblatt's articulation of new historicism launched the emergence, and some might say dominance, of the critical practice in the American academy. New historicism perceives literature as located within a historical, cultural, and social matrix and that this matrix allows for a deep reading of the text in question. At the same time, the scholar is to maintain a self-reflexive critical stance in relation to the text. While there is agreement on aspects of critical representation of the text, new historicists resisted a monolithic definition of their approach. In "The Historicist Enterprise," Jeffrey N. Cox and Larry J. Reynolds point to "sharp differences between the concerns and practices of various New Historicists." Regardless of dissension, they believe that "the enterprise has discernible features."[4] H. Aram Vesser pinpoints the following as central tenets of new historicism:

> 1) that every expressive act is embedded in a network of material practices; 2) that every act of unmasking, critique, and opposition uses the tools it condemns and risks falling

prey to the practice it exposes; 3) that literary and non-literary 'texts' circulate inseparably; 4) that no discourse, imaginative or archival, gives access to unchanging truths or expresses unalterable human nature; and 5) that a critical method and a language adequate to describe culture under capitalism participate in the economy they describe.[5]

Or, in Louis A. Montrose's definition:

> The writing and reading of texts, as well as the processes by which they are circulated and categorized, analyzed and taught, are being reconstructed as historically determined and determining modes of cultural work; apparently autonomous aesthetic and academic issues are being reunderstood as inextricably though complexly linked to other discourses and practices—such linkages constituting the social networks within which individual subjectivities and collective structures are mutually and continuously shaped.[6]

The shifting definitions remind us that new historicism is, as Greenblatt emphasizes, "a practice rather than a doctrine,"[7] and while those working within the boundaries of new historicism never fashioned a shared definition of the term, these interpretations suggest how we might imagine a coherent critical approach through which to analyze the digital archive.

Greenblatt may have launched our contemporary understanding of new historicism, but Jerome McGann brought new historicism to the digital age. Donald Waters, Andrew W. Mellon Foundation program officer, identifies McGann's 1983 *A Critique of Modern Textual Criticism* as the text that launched literary digital humanities.[8] Waters's assessment hinges on McGann's theory of textuality: McGann contends that "the apparitions of text—its paratexts, bibliographical codes, and all visual features—are as important in the text's signifying programs as the linguistic elements," and "that the social intercourse of texts—the *context* of their relations—must be conceived an essential part of the 'text itself' if one means to gain an adequate critical grasp of the textual situation."[9] In fact, McGann acknowledges that the theory of text articulated in his 1983 volume contributed to his decision to experiment with digital scholarship, but he believes that his introduction "to UNIX computing systems and to hypermedia" in the 1980s was equally as important. The emergence of new ideas regarding text and technology made McGann decide, "when circumstances were right I would undertake building a computerized hypermedia model for scholarly editing."[10]

McGann found the appropriate circumstances in 1993 when the University of Virginia launched the Institute for Advanced Technology in the Humanities (IATH) under John Unsworth's directorship. Unsworth's experience with the electronic journal, *Postmodern Culture*, convinced him that the open access, web-based delivery of materials, rather than the proprietary stand-alone CD-ROM used by the majority of the contemporary digital edition projects, was most suitable for IATH's digital projects.[11] One cannot overstate how important Unsworth's insistence on the web-based model would prove to the future of digital literary work, for without Unsworth's leadership we may well have continued to produce our digital projects on the CD-ROM, a form that has stymied digital textual editions production with issues including interoperability, speed of use, and limited storage size. McGann reminds us that Unsworth's web-based approach moved "against nearly every current in humanities computing scholarship, which was dominated by 'stand alone' ideas and technologies (epitomized in the early and short-sighted choice of CD-ROM as the venue for carrying humanities texts and hypertexts)."[12] The *RA* began as a small HTML prototype, what McGann labels "a kind of thought experiment."[13] Once the prototype was developed, the *RA* discussed expansion through a partnership with the University of Michigan Press. The project

Fig. 2.1. University of Michigan Press Catalog, fall 1999.

with the Press proceeded to the point where the website license for *The Complete Writings and Pictures of Dante Gabriel Rossetti: A Hypermedia Research Archive* was advertised in Michigan's fall 1999 catalogue and a site mock-up featured on the catalogue front page (see fig. 2.1).

The publishing relationship disintegrated when McGann insisted that the site be open access and extensible, an untenable financial arrangement for the Press. The *WWA* has a similar history. After an initial HTML prototype was developed, Price and his coeditor Ed Folsom worked with Primary Source Media to distribute a less robust version of selected materials as a CD collection titled *Major Authors on CD-ROM: Walt Whitman.*[14] Ultimately the *WWA* chose to proceed with a more robust, open access version of the archive. With their insistence on open access web-based projects, the *RA*, *WWA*, and other projects of their ilk launched new standards for digital literary studies.

As the digital archive form began to be replicated by other scholars, so too would the underlying theoretical model derived from new historicism. In 1993, when McGann launched his *Rossetti Archive*, he coined the term digital archive to describe his work and, in doing so, rejected the textual studies linked term digital edition that had driven digital humanities work during the previous period.[15] The archive offered possibilities that the book did not: "When a book is produced it literally closes its covers on itself," but archives, in McGann's mind, are "built so that its contents and its webwork of relations (both internal and external) can be indefinitely expanded and developed."[16] The web of relations is crucial to the archive form and is derived in large part from new historicist conceptions of the archive. Working in reaction to perceived limitations of new criticism and poststructuralist criticism, new historicists centered their research within the physical archive. Marjorie Levinson aptly calls new historicism "a kind of systems analysis,"[17] a statement oddly predictive of the way that computer technologies would be enacted in the digital archive and an emphasis on how archives became the sort of space in which the scholar would piece together textual interrelations. If an intervention into an archive is a sort of systems analysis, the intervention is also, in reference to Derrida's *Archive Fever*, a constructed and deconstructable entity. No archive can be "without outside."[18] Archival instability, a legacy of Derridian conceptions of power and truth, continues to inform the way that digital literary scholars understand the work we undertake. Nowhere is this more apparent than in the 2009 *DHQ* special cluster entitled "Done."[19] Underlying this special cluster is the insistence that digital works are highly mutable and perceptions of completeness are purely subjective. Brown et al. write, "'Doneness' circulates discursively within a complex and evolving scholarly ecology where new modes of digital publication are changing our conceptions of textuality, at the same time that models of publication, funding, and archiving are rapidly changing."[20] The multiple factors influencing the conception of completeness as well as the type of projects produced within the evolving parameters lend to the charge of instability. However, viewed within the new historicist legacy of Derridian archive, we might better understand why reading the archive through a complex set of power dynamics becomes more important than locking down a set of protocols of production.

The digital archive seems designed to meet the needs of the scholar interested in producing the "thick description" criticism central to new historicist work. Derived from anthropologist Clifford Geertz, thick description was the practice of "giving the act its place in a network of framing intentions and cultural meanings."[21] Thick description necessitated the examination of a broad selection of materials including literature, political documents, art, newspapers, material objects, and more, and new historicist scholars read materials from the Society for the Prevention of Premature Burial next to biblical texts and altar clothes.[22] Using "an empirically responsible investigation of the contemporary meanings informing literary works (their parts, their production, their reception), as well as other social texts," according to Marjorie Levinson, new historicists "regard these meanings as systematically interrelated within the period in question, but since we do not organize the system by a dynamic concept of ideology on the one hand, and of structural determination on the other, our inquires do not give rise to a meaningful historical sequence."[23] Levinson's catalog of parts, production, and reception harks back to book history approaches, but the emphasis on social texts as dynamic and indeterminate prepares the way for a world of bits and bites, of interrelated and indeterminate nodes of meaning. The digital environment would attempt to represent what Brook Thomas calls "a literary work's embeddedness within a larger system of textuality"[24] and could cross "the boundaries separating history, anthropology, art, politics, literature, and economics."[25] Certainly McGann saw the *RA* as a "self-reflexive system," a "laboratory to study books,"[26] and a reflection of social text theory. Even critics such as W. Speed Hill recognized that the *RA* was a natural outgrowth of McGann's theoretical approach:

> . . . if you forego the search for the single, authorially sanctioned, text-as-end-product-of-the-editorial-process, the logic of your position inexorably drives you beyond the codex and toward the archive. If meaning is dependent upon context, and contexts are multiple—indeed infinitive-only an infinitely extensible archive can contain the relevant data.[27]

In the heady days of digital archive development, the web seemed to provide a natural test bed for McGann's theoretical articulations and a new digital literary genre was born.

While the digital environment would allow experimentation with new historicist ideas, new historicism also afforded the digital authority. As discussed in the previous chapter, scholars were concerned that the digital space was seemingly unreliable, the antithesis of the peer reviewed, press-driven world of academic scholarship. How would those interested in producing digital materials resolve this problem? One of the means of shoring up the reputation of digital work was found in new historicism. "The practice of New Historicism," according to Sonja Laden," is also authorized by the archive, or the library, as a more or less official repository of records: at once a site for storing a variety of material artifacts and documents and . . . a metaphorical site of 'how people imagine what they know and what institutions validate that knowledge.'"[28] The choice of the term archive, then, does more than describe the gathered materials. The mimesis of the rare book archive, a form understood and given great value in scholarly circles, provides a means by which to bring value and authority to digital work. Influenced by Derrida's conception of the archive, new historicists well understood the way that their use of archive both as authority and construction gave weight to the work they commenced. Derrida's insistence that archives "inhabit this unusual place, this place of election where law and singularity intersect in *privilege*," and "[a]t the intersectional of the topological and the nomological, of the place and the law, of the substrate and the authority, a scene of domiciliation becomes once visible and invisible."[29] Derrida's conception of the archive as law and yet not may indeed point to why those working within new historicism were invested in digital archives. Such scholars understood that, like Derrida's archive, the new Internet age and the transfer of texts to digital forms were acts of authority, of fixing, and of "gathering together" to give form, while the process of creating such slippery human knowledge within computer code was impossible, the very deconstruction that Derrida insists upon.[30]

Derrida's reading of the archive underpins the modeling of the text in digital archives. New historicism treated texts "as objects and events in the world, as a part of human life, society, the historical realities of power, authority, and resistance,"[31] but, following Derrida's line of thinking, new historicism rejects absolutes. This duality is reflected in the digital archive's textual representation that rejects the sure codifications that were dominant in the earlier digital formulation of the edition. Eschewing genres that suggested power differentials within criticism, new historicist digital scholars rejected "literature" as the most valued term and flattened the categories "literature" and "historical document," instead adopting the broader category "digital object." While the term digital object is common in computer parlance (digital object architecture, digital object identifier), digital object is used far more loosely in digital literary studies, often slipping between object, text, image, and document, a slippage seemingly related to the digital archive's new historicist theoretical roots. While the digital edition utilized the simulacrum of the scanned page or art image, hence the high-quality digital images contained in archives such as the *RA* or *WWA*, those constructing the digital archive did not fetishize the image as was true in the earlier digital edition form. Instead, digital archives emphasized that "object" was a generalized concept much as new historicists used the term "text" to apply a lack of preference for form or genre or a baseline from which to begin criticism. Unsworth demonstrates his preference for the valueless digital object when he argues that "it is best if the authoritative name of a digital object has as little meaning as possible, and instead conveys the information we are tempted to load into the semantics of the name by some other means—for example, by breaking it out explicitly in different attribute values, or different database fields, or in some other way making it explicit rather than implied. The only thing one really wants a name to do, in short, is to distinguish this thing from other things, and so the only really required quality of a name—in the world of digital objects, at least—is uniqueness."[32] Unsworth's concern is with the best way to process a large number of related objects, but the emphasis on forcing a gap between meaning and object is crucial in this stage of digital production where the digital archive relegates the materiality of the text to an equal status as the social web of the texts, a very different position than that found in the digital edition where the image is primary.

The rejection of an object's individuated ascribed power is greatly influenced by the work of Foucault. A key figure in new historicist theorization, Foucault is interested, in the words of Stuart Hall, in "the relationship between knowledge and power, and how power operated within what he called an **institutional apparatus** and its **technologies** (techniques),"[33] ideas that form the foundation of how digital archivists understand the way by which texts and technologies interact and build knowledge within the archive. To Foucault, "The apparatus is thus always inscribed in a play of power, but it is also always linked to certain coordinates of knowledge which issue from it but, to an equal degree, condition it. This is what the apparatus consists in: strategies of relations of forces supporting, and supported by, types of knowledge."[34] Perhaps we should not be surprised that digital archives are imbued with Foucault's ideas of apparatus and his emphasis on techniques, roughly translated to technologies, though Foucault would not have imagined the impact of desktop computers when he was writing of such technologies. The digital archive balances an understanding of how the technologies, including the open access web, metadata, and interface, impact the understanding of an object, hence McGann's chiding of Ed Folsom's representation of the *WWA* in a *PMLA* issue focused on database.[35] McGann, echoing Foucault's understanding of apparatus, argues that "no database can function without a user interface, and in the case of cultural materials the interface is an especially crucial element of these kinds of digital instruments. Interface embeds, implicitly and explicitly, many kinds of hierarchical and narrativized organizations."[36] The insistence on reading the archive and its power broadly is also a call to balance materiality with meaning. Margaret Ezell emphasizes that the digital archive model must represent the materiality of the object intertwined in a social matrix, in effect creating a balancing act that preserves textuality through a systems approach; "That the very materiality of women's handwritten artifacts is its own system of textuality can easily be lost again in a system that privileges the linguistic."[37] Certainly the move away from an overemphasis on materiality that occurs in the digital archive period is influenced by the work of Foucault and other new historicists who reject narrow representations of meaning and object.

In 2005 NINES released Collex, the search and collection interface developed for its federated collection of nineteenth-century materials. The interface is a tribute to McGann's belief that technology is intimately enmeshed with social understandings of the materials it represents, and, as such, Collex enacts the theoretical representation of new historicism's journey into digital archive development. "A Ruby-On-Rails application," Collex "allows users to search aggregated sites, collect, annotate, and tag the online objects they discover, and to repurpose those objects in illustrated, interlinked essays or exhibits."[38] Collex allows users to explore peer reviewed scholarly projects, selected special collections library catalogs, and related commercial collections and journals. Yet Collex is far more than a mechanism to search through the collected NINES materials as it "*embodies* interpretive acts"[39] and facilitates the new historicist understanding of objects within a social system. Collex treats each object as an individual item, which allows the user to theorize relationships among the objects and to remix the archive accordingly. As users build relationships, Collex ingests the findings, recognizing "the contexts in which they <individual objects> are placed by a community of scholars."[40] At the same time, Collex transparently reveals the constructed nature of its network through its ever-shifting tags. Tags are user-generated words that describe objects found in NINES, modeled on the crowd sourcing uses of word clouds in sites from flickr to Delicious. As users attach tags to individual digital objects, such as scholarly articles, poems, or paintings, the word cloud and the search are altered, reminding the user that the objects exist within and are impacted by a scholarly community using the site (see fig. 2.2).

The manipulation of the digital archive materials through the Collex tool is akin to the use of a box of papers found in a special collections room. Grouped by subject, patrons pull various papers and objects from a box, ordering the items by interest and possible connectivity. As patrons finish with the materials they return them to the box in new constellations that represent interpretations. Unlike the earlier digital edition, where scholar-

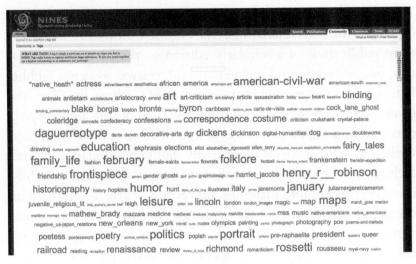

Fig. 2.2. NINES Collex tags in a word cloud.

creators worked to fix the original text to one meaning, digital archives reveal the social construction of meaning through interface, design, and use.

The lure of the rare book room echoes in the construction of digital archives from this period. At the heart of digital archive construction is the desire for immersion in a wide range of textual materials, what Kenneth Price calls "the ideal of . . . all-inclusive resources for the study of given topics."[41] New historicist scholars who perceived the archive as the space of scholarship viewed the digital as a tool for enacting the ideal of textual inclusion. For example, the *WWA* is premised on the problem of Whitman's manuscripts, "scattered in over sixty different institutional repositories, and poetry manuscripts have been located in twenty-nine repositories."[42] The construction of an inclusive digital archive would return the manuscripts to a central location, the *WWA*, and, even better, allow for additional materials to interact with Whitman's writing. Such concerns have led to the hallmark of digital archives, the ever-expanding archive.

The Willa Cather Archive (WCA), for example, has increasingly expanded the interrelated materials housed on its site, evolving from publication of a scholarly edition to the inclusion of letters, images, audio and movie clips, interviews, speeches, public letters, and a geographic representation of Cather's life. The organic archive, however, could quickly become the unbounded, never-ending digital project. Like new historicist work, often described as scholarship without easily defined boundaries, digital archives tend to be porous rather than restrictive. The possibility of ever-expanding materials, however, is a greater problem in the digital environment, where press conventions are not active, digital storage is capacious, and additions and corrections might continue indefinitely. Ed Folsom connects the expansiveness of the *WWA* to the huge, unfinished Whitman print project, the *Collected Writing of Walt Whitman*, noting that the editors of the *Collected Writing* "thought, just as Kenneth Price and I foolishly thought when we began the *Walt Whitman Hypertext Archive*, that they'd be done with the project in a few years."[43] What Folsom misunderstands, however, is that an edition of writings, whether print or digital, is far more contained than the idealized digital archive driven by the underlying principles of organicism and the unbounded understanding of the text. Developers of digital archives have attempted methods of border control, including the most common method, a focus on a particular author, period, or geographic location, but most archives continue to struggle with material selection.

Digital archivists were also impacted by the newly expanded canon, in part a result of new historicist work invested in revaluing texts for their historical and cultural impact rather than just literary style. Such scholarship brought works by Charlotte Perkins Gilman, Kate Chopin, and Harriet Beecher Stowe, among many others, into a far broader canon than existed during the new critical period, leaving digital archivists further concerned with how to delineate boundaries for archive construction. In fact, the impact of canon expansion might be traced from print to digital in a number of early archives, including Stephen Railton's *Uncle Tom's Cabin & American Culture*. Jane Tompkins's 1985 book *Sensational Designs* successfully argued for the central position of *Uncle Tom's Cabin* in the nineteenth-century American canon. Re-situating sentimental fiction as an important form of literary production and one worthy of study, Tompkins drew upon contemporary feminist and new historicist work, arguing that "novels and stories should be studied not because they manage to escape the limitations of their particular time and place, but because they offer powerful examples of the way a culture thinks about itself, articulating and proposing solutions for the problems that shape a particular historical moment."[44] The importance of *Uncle Tom's Cabin* and similar sentimental fictional texts is not found in their literary value, claimed Tompkins, but in what the texts reveal about the culture from which they came. The job of the literary critic, then, is to examine the multiple threads of history and culture in which the text is produced, providing deep readings that reveal new insight into the text. Rejecting the formalist reading of literature, "stylistic intricacy, psychological subtlety, epistemological complexity," Tompkins sets *Uncle Tom's Cabin* within a web, and here I use the term in all of its multiple meanings, of cultural and historical materials.[45] Stephen Railton's *Uncle Tom's Cabin & American Culture* reiterates the new historicist argument in digital form by situating Stowe's text within a network of cultural and historical texts, digitally enacting Tompkins's argument. Produced at the University of Virginia in partnership with the Electronic Text Center, Special Collections Alderman Library, IATH, and the Harriet Beecher Stowe Center, the site compiles cultural materials that illustrate the centrality of Stowe's text to nineteenth-century culture. Called a "Multi-Media Archive," the site includes various versions of *Uncle Tom* novels, images, songs, tracts, critical essays, reviews, adapted plays, songs, and movies. Organized around responses to and adaptations of the novel, the archive represents a place in which a scholar might conduct broad and deep historical and cultural research, the hallmark of the digital archive moment. While Railton does not identify as a new historicist, there is every indication that new historicism informs the materials selection and that the archive argues for the importance of *Uncle Tom's Cabin*, the novel, using the same criteria as Tompkins's scholarly work. Where Tompkins's scholarship points to the centrality of the sentimental novel, Railton's archive includes a number of pretexts from sentimental culture. Where Tompkins's scholarship points to the centrality of religious piety, Railton's archive includes Christian texts. Railton even extends Tompkins's argument for the cultural standing of *Uncle Tom's Cabin* by including multiple responses to the text, such as reviews and adaptations, and by creating an archive where the selected materials show the significance of the novel within Stowe's contemporary culture.

No matter that the idealized digital archive was expansive, the signature style of new historicism, the anecdote, reinforced the continued centrality of the individual item. Peppered throughout new historicist scholarship, the anecdote "is drawn from diverse archival disciplines . . . [and is] placed alongside authorial 'culturally sanctioned' literary texts."[46] Anecdotes range from a painting read against a Shakespeare play to a bawdy broadside illuminating a religious text, with the anecdote reinforcing the new historicist belief in "the value of the single voice, the isolated scandal, the idiosyncratic vision, the transient sketch."[47] However, the new historicist commitment to viewing the object or the anecdote within a larger connective social web created an unresolved tension between the individual and the collective that would be replicated in digital archives. Scholars developing digital archives idealized organic and expansive datasets but faced limitations including economics, scale, and form that have limited the produced archives to the point where the final product might be read as a collection of anecdotes. Instead of seeing the contradiction as insurmountable, scholars such as Alan Liu view the anecdote as a form of "random access. If the new historicism is a kind of relational database, then the anecdote is its query."[48] Anecdotes might be seen as the way into history, as "the random anecdote's interior contradiction, irony, or aporia . . . exposes the fault lines in the 'reality' of history itself." In its digital version, "New Historicism is the intuition simultaneously of random access (an atheist transcendent) *and* determination (a bowing down or conviction)."[49] Though the anecdote might appear limiting, even retrograde, Liu's analysis situates it as a wedge through which to view the moments that do not fit, the space in which scholars might successfully probe for new findings.

Perhaps the most enduring legacy of new historicism is digital literary studies' rejection of the innate meaning of both individual objects and the structures in which they function. New historicists scrutinized form and materials, studied what was in and out of the archive, and questioned the power relations formed by the construction of and use of the archive. If new historicism is distinguished "by its lack of faith in 'objectivity' and 'permanence' and its stress not upon the direct recreation of the past, but rather the processes by which the past is constructed or invented,"[50] so too are digital archives characterized by the same. Scholars who engage in digital archive creation also refused to view the archive and the technology used to create it as naturalized or organic and remained self-reflexive about all aspects of the archive, from materials selection, to metadata, and to interface design. Writing about *The Women Writers Project*, Margaret Ezell underscores that "how archives are put together, maintained, and accessed affects the stories that are told about them and the stories that their contents tell."[51] Technologies used to create archives, such as TEI/XML, the de facto metadata standard in digital literary studies, have been carefully dissected.[52] New historicist insistence on social construction bleeds into the way scholars understand metadata and the encoding of texts. Martha Nell Smith is clear that the TEI is not a naturalized computer code but a socially produced form impacted by cultural and social values; "Meeting the challenge [of encoding texts] requires asking in as many ways as can be imagined how to go about reckoning the hierarchies apparently accepted by coding for rendering the images and texts in digital format, hierarchies that stubbornly resist parity between the intellectual/textual object and physical object but that insist one must be subordinate to the other."[53] We should not underestimate the importance of such an understanding of self-reflexivity, as it provides a methodological means for digital humanities to focus on a broad set of theoretical engagements from critical code studies to datamining. The notion of a scholar's purview as broad and diverse, interconnected and social rather than limited to a particular author or literary text, crucially influences the direction of digital literary studies. As digital archivists began to interrogate code and connectivity they were implicitly arguing for an expansion of study akin to the interdisciplinary interests of new historicism, or the big tent of digital humanities.

As this analysis demonstrates, the impact of new historicism on the theoretical and structural conceptualization of the digital archive is foundational to the way that literary digital humanities has evolved. However, one crucial, muted issue that has deep roots in the new historicist past continues to plague the evolving field—the growing hostility between literature and history scholars working within the digital environment. David Parry's post on his *AcademHack* blog provides one example of this tension:

> Digital Historians have leveraged the digital to expand and engage a wider public in the work of history. As examples of this think of Omeka, or leveraging social media to engage in crowd sourced projects. That is, Digital Historians have often begun by asking "how does the digital allow us to reach a larger/public audience?" Now this could be because many of the folks working in Digital

History come from a public history background . . . But in the case of literary studies the "digital" projects have not, as much, changed the scope of the audience. So that if you look at digital literary projects they often look remarkably similar to projects in the pre-digital era, just ones which have been put on steroids and run thru a computational process. Seems to me that the Digital Historian model is a better one.[54]

We might dismiss Parry's post as symptomatic of academic Balkanism, yet the expressed division between literature and history scholars is not an isolated incident. Historian Edward Ayers has stated, "The irony is that history may be better suited to digital technology than any other humanistic discipline."[55] To historians like Dan Cohen, digital work is most appropriate for history because of scholarly approach. Cohen posits,

> We need to recognize that the digital humanities represent a scary, rule-breaking, swashbuckling movement for many historians and other scholars. We must remember that these scholars have had—for generations and still in today's graduate schools—a very clear path for how they do their work, publish, and get rewarded. Visit archive; do careful reading; find examples in documents; conceptualize and analyze; write monograph; get tenure. We threaten all of this. For every time we focus on text mining and pattern recognition, traditionalists can point to the successes of close reading—on the power of a single word. We propose new methods of research when the old ones don't seem broken.[56]

On the one hand, Cohen's representation of the threat of digital humanities rings true. New approaches to research create tension within scholarly fields, particularly as scholars must learn new techniques. Situating the archive as a central trope in the battle over digital humanities, Cohen suggests that the close reading approach, "the power of a single word," is a traditionalist methodology not appropriate for the new digital form.[57] However, as the previous discussion of both the archive and the edition reveals, close attention to individual objects, such as the word, remains a guiding principle in digital literary studies. While the data driven model has much to offer scholarship, those that come to the digital from a new historicist background are suspicious of a monolithic use of data, not because it is data but because the individual moment, which can become occluded in such a data dump, has the power to rewrite and disrupt the larger narrative only when it is located by a scholar through an interpretive moment. To digital literary scholars, the uniqueness or individuality of an object needs to be understood as potentially disrupting the larger context, rather than a piece that is always viewed within a continuous narrative. Here Alan Liu's understanding of the anecdote as random access in a database is illuminating, as the anecdote allows disruption through "the single word," the very object that Cohen dismisses. The dangerous trend toward the homogenization of digital work in the supposed interdisciplinary digital humanities masks the methodological concerns that promote such differences and needs to be resisted as the broader digital humanities develops.

If the digital humanities are interdisciplinary, why the continued conflicts between history and literature? The history of interdisciplinarity in the academy provides one means of reading the dislocation. Joe Moran's *Interdisciplinarity* traces the rise of disciplines from Aristotle through current academic structures and contends that, "Broadly speaking, the development of disciplines has not merely created self-contained bodies of knowledge, happy in their isolation; it has been accompanied by frequent attempts to assert the superiority of certain fields of learning over others."[58] Moran's "self-contained bodies" that house interdisciplinary thought provide a means of understanding the fraught relationship of history and literature. If digital interdisciplinarity is based on traditional assumptions of multi-disciplinary knowledge housed within one body, then hierarchical tensions surely will occur. Far more productive is the emphasis on interdisciplinarity built through collaboration. It is also likely that the struggle between history and literature might be more fraught than other disciplines because of the two disciplines' historical emergence:

> The two subjects were sometimes taught together in early degrees at dissenting colleges in the nineteenth century, and they developed as fully-fledged academic subjects at around the same time. Each of these disciplines contains elements of the other: literary studies often draws on historical material, while everything, including literature, could be said to have a history. The obvious connections between the subjects, however, have not always encouraged co-operation; they have often led to greater territoriality, as each subject has sought to consolidate its own separateness and uniqueness.[59]

The tensions between history and literature are nothing new, according to Moran, yet certain periods heighten the anxiety. New historicism was one such moment where clashes between literature and history peaked, and the new age of digital archive work seems to have reignited the battle.

Yet we need to recognize that the reason disciplinary tension appears in contemporary discussions is because disciplines still matter. Disciplines govern our academic lives, from our graduate training, to our position in the university, to the type of work valued, to our ability to advance in our careers. Universities continue to organize knowledge groups into traditional subject areas, so it should come as no surprise that we find it difficult to work outside our traditional structures. If we agree that one scholar cannot move intellectually across all disciplinary fields, then we must learn how to use the generalized umbrella term of digital humanities to bring together scholars from multiple fields. One of the strengths of the broad digital humanities is its ability to pull together diversely trained scholars, as "there may be human intellectual limits to interdisciplinarity: given that most research in the humanities is undertaken by scholars working on their own, it may be difficult for these people to become conversant in the theories, methods and materials of two or more disciplines, without producing significant gaps in their knowledge."[60] We pretend that disciplinary boundaries have ceased to exist at our peril. Instead of shying away from such complexities, we should embrace the heady dissention. While the old/new historicist split created controversy rather than interdisciplinary cooperation, it also generated intellectual stimulation and fertile ground for experimentation. This tension between fields could prove fruitful for digital scholarship, generating new intellectual questions. Moran cautions that "[m]any of the examples of interdisciplinarity I have examined so far represent a kind of nostalgia for the lost unity of knowledge, and they see the discipline of English as the best way of restoring this."[61] By shifting interdisciplinarity out of one body to many bodies, by rejecting a coherence of approach, we may move away from the seduction of unity. To model interdisciplinarity, we must reject calls to lock down digital humanities to a particular methodology, instead privileging a broad range of approaches.

The archival turn in American digital literary work has created a theoretical foundation of use and analysis that underpins our current work. The construction of digital archives has brought cohesion to the field and allowed for the development of standardized approaches to the work that literary digital scholars are interested in undertaking. Yet, we need to remember that new historicism has taught us that the archive is our construction. Without careful attention to the way in which the archive structure itself represents our theoretical approach we have done a disservice to the possibility of digital work as more than just technique or application. As Louis Montrose wrote during the height of new historicism: "Inhabiting the discursive spaces traversed by the term 'New Historicism' are some of the most complex, persistent, and unsettling of the problems that professors of literature attempt variously to confront or to evade."[62] The scholarly complexity articulated by Montrose remains persistent and valid in contemporary digital studies. As Caroline Steedman reminds us of physical archives, "The Archive is not potentially made up of *everything*, as is human memory; and it is not the fathomless and timeless place in which nothing goes away that is the unconscious. The Archive is made from selected and consciously chosen documentation from the past and also from the mad fragmentations that no one intended to preserve and that just ended up there."[63] As our new historicist forerunners have taught, the digital archive has the potential to disrupt and fragment, even as it provides coherence and the most productive scholarship works within these gaps.

The central position maintained by digital archives in the late 1990s and early 2000s is diminishing. Fewer digital projects are adopting the term archive, and scholars are turning their attentiveness to datamining and geospatial representations. Yet the archive remains an important form that those working within the field must engage, as it strengthened the reputation of digital scholarship and laid the theoretical foundation for current work. We will continue to see projects that are best developed in the digital archive form, much as we continue to see digital editions. Yet there are new trends in digital literary studies that must also be tested and examined as we move forward.

CHAPTER 3

What's In and What's Out?

Digital Canon Cautions

Cyberspace is an environment comprised entirely of o's and
1's: simple binary switches that are either off or on. No in-
between. No halfway. No shades of gray. All too often, when
it comes to virtual culture, the subject of race seems to be one
of those binary switches: either it's completely "off" (i.e., race
is an invisible concept because it's simultaneously unmarked
and undiscussed), or it's completely "on" (i.e., it's a contro-
versial flashpoint for angry debate and overheated rhetoric).
While there are similar patterns of silence about race when
it comes to interpersonal interaction in "the real world," the
presence of visual and aural markers of race (no matter how
inaccurate those may be) means that race is rarely (if ever) as
invisible offline as it is in cyberspace.

 —Beth E. Kolko, Lisa Nakamura, and Gilbert B. Rodman,
  Introduction to *Race in Cyberspace*, Routledge, 2000, 1

In 2010, I located Sharon Harris's *Early American Women Writers*
website. By 2011, the site had been removed.

As the previous chapters chronicle, scholars working in the early
period of digital literary production experimented with delivery,
forms of access, interfaces, and representations of materiality.
The digital edition and digital archive models were successfully

replicated leading to a period of rapid digital production. Working within these models, a subset of scholars focused on what I dub "digital recovery projects," archives and editions that used digitization to expand what such scholars saw as an outmoded new critical literary canon that excluded work by women, people of color, queers, and others. Digital recovery projects emerged out of activist cultural studies communities and were tied to evolving understandings of the emergent Internet.

In the 1970s and 1980s, canon expansion was the literary holy grail. Groundbreaking scholarship, such as *The Madwoman in the Attic* by Gilbert and Gubar, argued for a broader canon, heralding a new generation of scholars that would begin to edit and publish previously excluded writers.[1] But scholarly presses had limited budgets and numerous texts remained unpublished or out of print, rejected because they were deemed noncommercially viable. Further, scholars of African American, Asian American, Native American, and Latino/a literatures charged that the white feminist movement had not sufficiently attended to writers of color. Among the most influential texts that attracted criticism was the Gilbert and Gubar *Norton Anthology of Literature by Women* (1985), condemned for its lack of women writers of color, divergent classes, and pre-1800 women's writing.[2] Scholars charged that the *Norton Anthology* had created an alternative canon that was as problematic as the previous canon that had excluded women's writing. Margaret Ezell's influential *Writing Women's Literary History* (1993), for example, articulates how "structures used to shape our narrative of women's literary history may have unconsciously continued the existence of the restrictive ideologies that initially erased the vast majority of women's writings from literary history and teaching texts."[3] One remedy to what was seen as a continued exclusionary canon was the launch of activist presses such as the Feminist Press (1970) and the Kitchen Table: Women of Color Press (1980), dedicated to publishing materials that mainstream and even scholarly presses were not printing.

Despite valiant efforts by activist presses and the increased publication of "lost" texts by mainstream and scholarly presses, it was clear that such efforts alone would not solve the canonical elisions. Dissatisfied, scholars and activists began to look for other solutions to solve the canon problem.

In the 1990s, proponents of the Internet began to tout the developing technological infrastructure as a tool to democratize knowledge. Popular culture portrayed the early 1990s Internet as an idealized, democratic, and free space that needed protection from the corporate market forces intent upon invading the open space theretofore dominated by scientists, hackers, and geeks. Advocates of the free web championed three ideas: "1) Access to computers should be unlimited and total; 2) All information should be free; (and) 3) Mistrust authority and promote decentralization," all ideas designed to allow "bubbles" of information to rise from the bottom, sowing "seeds of revolutionary change."[4] Scholars, too, began to understand the net as a space that altered power structures. As Paul Delany reports,

> The Internet has thus mutated into an unforeseen and unplanned information space. Its virtues can all be attributed to its collegial political economy: in a word, its openness. Internet's most important features are its relatively small hardware investment, a weak (but not ineffective) central administration, little censorship, and an absence of specifiable "bottom-line" objectives. Its explosive growth in the last few years confirms the dynamism of a collegial cyberspace culture in which millions of users exchange information, collaborate on creative projects, and have their say on any subject they care about.[5]

For scholars interested in challenging the traditional canon, the technological possibilities were a boon. It was imagined that the web would allow those previously cut off from intellectual capital to gain knowledge that might be leveraged to change their social position and would allow those who had been silenced to have a voice. Hypertext theorist Jay David Bolter, for example, promoted the freeing power of the web-based environment as a space that encouraged "the abandonment of the ideal of high culture (literature, music, the fine arts) as a unifying force. If there is no single culture, but only a network of interest groups, then there is no single favored literature or music."[6] The belief in the low cost of Internet-based publication would encourage scholars to embrace the Internet as a vehicle for disseminating cultural materials. In 1996, Peter Shillingsburg anticipated that it "eventually will cost less to produce and therefore, one assumes, to purchase a compact disk than it cost to produce and purchase Hans Gabler's edition of *Ulysses*."[7] In hindsight, Shillingsburg and the larger scholarly community have rejected this view as naïve and unrealistic, yet it was a common refrain in the early, heady days of digital recovery, where the faith in the Internet's ability to shift hierarchical structures became part of the narrative that in no small part drove the proliferation of digital literary recovery projects.

From the mid-1990s through the mid-2000s there was an explosion of digital sites that championed work previously excluded from the canon, what I label digital literary recovery projects.[8] Scholars worked individually or as small collectives to produce bibliographies or to publish primary texts. Simple HTML projects, such as *The 19th Century American Women Writers Web* (*19CWWW*), *Voices from the Gaps*, *Early American Women Writers*, *The Black Poetry Page*, *The Online Archive of Nineteenth-Century U.S. Women's Writings*, and *American Women Writers 1890 to 1939—Modernism and Mythology*,[9] were developed by scholars without the support of a digital humanities center, technological collaborators, or external funding. The activist recovery projects of this period were positioned to critique and respond to perceived weaknesses in the existing canon. Projects during this period were created using HTML, HyperText Markup Language, in large part because HTML was a fairly simple to learn tagging system that became even easier to use with the development of early HTML editors, including Claris Home Page, Mozilla Composer, and Adobe PageMill, all of which allowed novices to easily publish their findings. Sites built during this period were largely labors of love launched by scholars interested in disseminating materials that they found buried in difficult to access rare book rooms, crumbling newspapers, and unknown journals.

Such work envisages digital literary scholarship as a tool that might be utilized to meet the theoretical demands of scholarly work that reinserted women, queers, and people of color into the canon. For example, groundbreaking feminist scholar Judith Fetterley, whose 1978 *The Resisting Reader: A Feminist Approach to American Fiction* did much to challenge the traditional literary canon, nurtured a small online digital project to bring scholarly attention to the huge numbers of nineteenth-century women's texts that deserve critical scrutiny. Fetterley's personal website at the University of Albany, from which she is now retired, includes several pages of bibliographies and chronologies of what were then little known literary texts by American women.[10] Titled the *19th-Century Bibliography Project*, the site includes bibliography entries focused on women writers from the 1820s and 1830s arranged chronologically and alphabetically (see fig. 3.1).

Developed by students in a graduate course that Fetterley taught in 1995 and then compiled and published on the web by her student, Annie (formerly Lois Dellert) Raskin, Fetterley viewed the project as both pedagogical and activist. Articulating similar concerns about the canon as Ezell, Fetterley explains that:

> Underlying this project was the desire to make clear to students that the texts available for such a course as this represent only a fragment of the total work of women writers during the period, and that we are as much in danger of

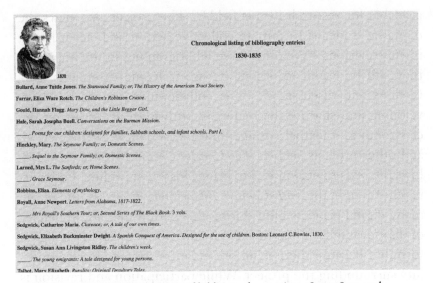

Fig. 3.1. Chronological listing of bibliography entries: 1830–1835. 19th-Century Bibliography Project. Judith Fetterley and Annie Raskin.

developing a skewed version of American literary history if we look only at the texts by women that have been reprinted in the last twenty years as we are if we look only at the work of male writers. In other words, the category of the "marginalized" can seem quite privileged when set in the context of a category that might well be called "the not-yet-marginalized."[11]

The online bibliography was a means of enacting a broader canon than that represented in print and is also indicative of the many such early digital projects where self-publication was designed to distribute work in progress, expand the literary and historical record, and spur new interest in the recovered texts. Unlike a print bibliography, which purports to be an authoritative, complete, and static overview of a particular author or topic, the *19th-Century Bibliography Project* is understood to be incomplete, in effect "an introduction to the various bibliographic resources available for research in this field."[12] The project also views the digital as a means to initiate collective action and, accordingly, invites revisions: "We offer these bibliographies in the hope that they will be useful to others and we welcome comments, corrections and discussion."[13] The collaborative approach to developing and sharing the materials, with Fetterley utilizing the classroom as a textual cottage industry, is typical of this period, and other projects such as *The Charles Chesnutt Archive* also follows the pedagogical model to bring "lost" texts online. Unfortunately, though, the *19th-Century Bibliography Project* is one of the many digital projects built during this period that are in danger of disappearance. The project is fragile not because of its digital form but because there is no preservation strategy nor community surrounding the project. While participation and revision is invited, there is no indication that the materials found in the bibliography had more than perhaps a revision or two. Published in 1996, the pages were last updated in 1997 and are now static and even decaying, an emblem of the larger state of digital recovery projects from this period.

In hindsight the limitations of recovery projects are clear, but for scholars interested in reworking the canon in the late 1990s, the web seemed a space of possibility. Scholars believed that the digital environment prevented presses and editors from limiting the types of work published. "What is new in the twenty-first century," writes Susan Fraiman, "is that now the guest list of history-making women is electronic—and there are always more seats at the table."[14] The belief in the Internet as a means to break the canon was likewise espoused by the editors of *Romantic Circles*: "One of the strengths of Web publishing is that it facilitates—even favors—the production of editions of texts and resources of so-called non-canonical authors and works."[15] Like Fraiman, the editors of *Romantic Circles* laud web publishing's ability to allow the scholar to work outside traditional publication mechanisms and to create expansive canons. The editors go on to identify the simplicity of digital publication as a key component of the success of the web. Success "is in part a function of the relative simplicity of HTML (and all of the simpler document-type-descriptions of SGML) and of 'workstation publishing' in general when compared to traditional commercial or academic letterpress production and distribution methods."[16] The ease of publication identified by the editors was what allowed the broad range of small-scale recovery projects to explode in this early period, as most of the projects were produced using simple hand coding of HTML or HTML editing programs. Digital recovery project URLs reveal that creators of projects often "published" their materials on personal webspace allotted by colleges and universities to their faculty and students. Technologically inexperienced users could create a simple textual project using low cost and low expertise methods, an approach contradictory to much of contemporary digital project development that tends to be conducted with the more complicated TEI/XML, databases, tools, and even datamining and algorithmic approaches. The low threshold at this moment of digital literary studies resulted in a broader set of textual materials being created and a democratic digital development.

Tracking the rise of the queercore, riot grrrl, and straight edge punk movements in the late 1980s and early 1990s provides one lens through which to read the digital literary studies movement. Emerging from 1970s punk, queercore, riot grrl, and straight edge punk movements adopted self-publication as activist interventions. Amy Spencer describes the riot grrl movement as "about using anything you can get your hands on to shape your own cultural entity; your own version of whatever is missing in mainstream culture,"[17] an ideology replicated in digital recovery projects from the mid to late 1990s. As did those interested in the digital recovery of texts, activist oriented music refused to rely on traditional methods of artistic dispersal, instead creating a self-publishing movement that allowed participants to create a broader canon of artistic expression. Riot grrl self-publication gave voice to the excluded:

> BECAUSE us girls crave records and books and fanzines that speak to US that WE feel included in and can understand in our own ways. BECAUSE we wanna make it easier for girls to see/hear each other's work so that we can share strategies and criticize-applaud each other. BECAUSE we must take over the means of production in order to create our own moanings. BECAUSE viewing our work as being connected to our girlfriends-politics-real lives is essential if we are gonna figure out how we are doing impacts, reflects, perpetuates, or DISRUPTS the status quo.[18]

Embracing a personal is political approach, both groups made visible excluded women, people of color, and queers—whether the exclusion was at a punk show, in print culture, in the classroom, or on a music label. The notion of such work as "underground" was vitally important, as the groups positioned their work against that of the dominant society. If mainstream record companies wouldn't sign queer singers, then singers would produce and distribute their work directly to fans. If scholarly publishers refused to print a relocated women's text, then scholars would create and publish the materials on the web for use by those interested.

Often localized and idiosyncratic, both movements were able to use new models of technology to promote inclusion and share understandings of voice and power through do-it-yourself (DIY) production of materials. Moore and Mitchel argue, "We see the DIY mechanism as both a relational mechanism because it both 'alters connections between people, groups, and networks,' which creates solidarities, and as a 'cognitive mechanism,' because it 'operates through alterations of individual and collective perception' by providing a foundation for the creation of imagined communities via taste and aesthetic choice."[19] A hallmark of the

DIY literary recovery projects is the development of a virtual community through various linking strategies. Projects often referenced other like-minded recovery projects through a list of links, creating an ever-expanding virtual network. For example, the *Native Web* included a list of authors, writers, and biographies (see fig. 3.2).

Native Web is activist in construction, community-focused in orientation, with a primary goal "to foster communication among peoples engaged in the present,"[20] a common thread in such digital recovery work. The importance of what I call "curated hyperlinked" sites has been unremarked upon by digital humanities scholars, a remnant of late 1990s web culture that now seem simplistic and out of date. Yet such work was pivotal to the formation of digital literary culture. Influential curated hyperlinked sites of the period include Alan Liu's *The Voice of the Shuttle* and Randy Bass's *The American Studies Crossroads Project.* [21] Donna Campbell's *American Writers* project provides an excellent example of curated hyperlinked projects used to construct a community of scholars interested in revising canons[22] (see figs. 3.2 and 3.3).

Launched in 1997, Campbell created the website to support a literature class. Housed on her personal webspace at Gonzaga University, the site grouped materials by author, time period, and literary movement. Historical, cultural, and biographical materials are also included as are links to primary texts.[23] Campbell's curated hyperlink site and others like it were developed to renegotiate canonical boundaries. Hence, the *American Writers* author list is far more diverse than contemporary anthologies, including little studied women, Native American, Latino/a, African American, and Asian American writers. Rather than devaluing such sites as technologically simplistic, we must resituate curated hypertext sites as crucial genres in the evolution of digital literary studies.

Open access, the use of digital technologies to distribute scholarly materials without cost or restriction, is also forecast in the 1990s digital recovery movement. For example, Kim Wells's

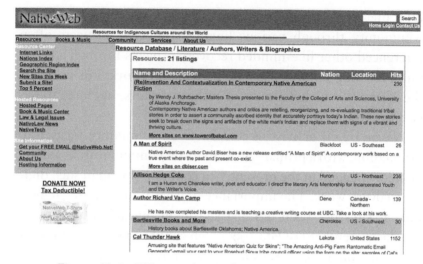

Fig. 3.2. *Native Web* screenshot, Authors, Writers & Biographies.

Home | Literary Movements | Timeline | American Authors | American Literature Sites

Gertrude Simmons Bonnin (Zitkala-Sa) (1876-1938)

Zitkala-Sa: Secondary Bibliography

Zitkala-Sa Biography and links at the Native American Authors Project
Biography by Roseanne Hoefel and bibliography at the The Online Archive of Nineteenth-Century U.S. Women's Writings. (Image courtesy of this site.)
Biographical sketch by Melessa Rae Henderson at the Voices from the Gaps: American Women of Color site. (New URL)

Kristin Herzog's general commentary on teaching Zitkala-Sa from the Heath Anthology site.
General Bibliography of Native American Literature

Works Available Online

Page images from the *Atlantic Monthly* new!

- Impressions of an Indian Childhood (January 1900)
- School Days of an Indian Girl (February 1900)
- An Indian Teacher among Indians (March 1900)

An Indian Teacher Among Indians *Atlantic Monthly* (1900), Volume 85.
Impressions of an Indian Childhood *Atlantic Monthly* 85 (1900): 37-47.
Old Indian Legends (1901)
Old Indian Legends at Project Gutenberg
School Days of an Indian Girl *Atlantic Monthly* 85 (1900): 185-94.
Soft Hearted Sioux *Harper's Monthly*, New York (1901)
The Trial Path *Harper's Monthly*, Volume 103, October 1901 .
"A Warrior's Daughter" (1902)
"Why I Am a Pagan" by Zitkala Sa *Atlantic Monthly* 90 (1902): 801-803.

Timeline ⬍ Go

Fig. 3.3. Zitkala Sa page, *American Writers* curated hyperlinked site.

Domestic Goddess website, which focused on canonically excluded women writers,[24] positioned open access and education as central goals of digital recovery projects:

> I think it is our duty as teachers not to ignore the possibilities of making research easily available on the Internet. If educators do not provide the information, who will? Do students have to pay for it, as a lot of encyclopedia companies are requiring now? This makes information only commercial, and even if they buy a subscription, sometimes the information they get is incomplete, and encyclopedic, rather than critical. These sites are great—but *I* want to teach for free.[25]

The desire to educate and freely disperse information is apparent in other early sites, including Kristin Mapel-Bloomberg's *American Women Writers 1890–1939*, *Modernism and Mythology*, and Shari Benstock's *Women of the Left Bank*, all of which publish supplemental scholarly materials to their accompanying print books.[26] Such work, tied to DIY activist movements that bled into scholarship, is among the earliest representation of open source scholarly publishing and, like curated hyperlinked texts, needs to be reconfigured within the history of digital literary studies. Though often dismissed as simplistic or unimportant, open source distribution of materials brought attention to writers that had not been represented in the canon and helped to launch our current understanding of public scholarship.

As individual scholars began to share recovered texts online, libraries began to explore how they might use the digital to bring their collections to a larger audience. Etext centers were started at Rutgers University and Princeton University (Center for Electronic Texts in the Humanities [CETH]), the University Library of the University of North Carolina at Chapel Hill (*Documenting the American South*), the University of Virginia (The Electronic

Text Center [Etext]), and other universities. [27] Some of the centers emphasized out-of-print and recovery texts, as was the case with the University of North Carolina's *Documenting the American South*, but most were focused on the digitization of canonical texts. The UVA Etext Center is arguably the most important center during this period due to the quality and quantity of the projects they produced,[28] as well as the students trained within the center who include notable contemporary digital scholars Stephen Ramsay, David Gants, Lisa Spiro, Tanya Clement, Matthew Kirschenbaum, and Amanda French. The Center digitized a broad assortment of texts, recovered and traditional; noncanonical texts by Native American, African Americans, and women writers coexisted with Founding Father documents by Thomas Jefferson and Alexander Hamilton. While the bulk of the texts that the Center digitized were selected by Etext staff from the UVA library stacks, a type of pre-Google digitization project, individual scholars would also suggest targeted texts of interest, including many of the noncanonical texts, for digitization. Virginia's Etext Center was unusual in its digitization of noncanonical texts as most other centers, according to Mandell and Gamer, were traditional in their approach: "the web—at least in its first stages—did reproduce canonical biases long inscribed in Romantic poetry. This was particularly true of 'early' electronic text collections, like those compiled at Oxford, Toronto, Berkeley, and Carnegie Mellon, to name a few."[29] Those centers that produced noncanonical texts shared a common focus on faculty and graduate student input in text selection. Scholarly participation, therefore, was a central factor in the selection of texts digitized during this period.

One successful recovery collaboration between an etext center, the University of Virginia, and an individual scholar, Jean Lee Cole, was the *Winnifred Eaton Digital Archive (WEDA)*[30] (see fig. 3.4).

Immediately after publishing her 2002 book on Eaton, *The Literary Voices of Winnifred Eaton: Redefining Ethnicity and Au-*

The Winnifred Eaton Digital Archive
Edited & Compiled by Jean Lee Cole
Assistant Professor, Department of English
Loyola College in Maryland

Hosted & Maintained by the Electronic Text Center
University of Virginia Library

I Home I Browse I Search I

About the archive

Winnifred Eaton (1875-1954), writing under the pseudonym of Onoto Watanna, was the first person of Asian descent to publish a novel in the U.S. (*Miss Numè of Japan,* 1898; available in a reprint edition edited by Eve Oishi [Johns Hopkins UP, 1999]). Perhaps more significantly, she was the first Asian American to reach a national mainstream reading audience: between 1898 and 1925, she published over a dozen novels, most of them with Harper and Brothers, and dozens of short stories and non-fiction pieces, which appeared in mass-market periodicals such as *Ladies' Home Journal, Frank Leslie's Popular Monthly, Century Magazine,* and *Harper's Monthly.* Her second novel, *A Japanese Nightingale* (1901; available in a reprint edition edited by Jean Lee Cole and Maureen Honey [Rutgers UP, 2002]), sold hundreds of thousands of copies and was adapted for both Broadway and film. According to the testimony of surviving family members and Winnifred Eaton herself, the number of her periodical publications may have neared or surpassed a hundred works. However, scholars until now have only located twenty short stories and about a dozen non-fiction pieces; a number of these have been recently anthologized in *The Half-Caste and Other Writings* (2003), edited by Linda Trinh Moser and Elizabeth Rooney.

None of the texts collected here appear in *The Half-Caste and Other Writings* or in any other anthology that includes Eaton's works. They thus greatly expand the known output of this important early figure in Asian American literature. The archive includes short stories, short fiction pieces, and complete novels, all of which appear in popular magazines of the period including *American Home Journal* (later renamed *Conkey's Home*

Fig. 3.4. *Winnifred Eaton Digital Archive,* screenshot.

thenticity (Rutgers University Press), Cole uncovered numerous "lost" Eaton stories and novels. Unable to secure a publisher for the little known author's work (publication of Eaton's work was not commercially viable, according to the presses she contacted), Cole explored other options for publication. When she attended the Rare Book School at the University of Virginia, Cole was put in touch with the Etext Center to discuss the possible digital publication of the materials.[31] Cole created a digital archive housed on the UVA Etext Center servers that included an introduction to Eaton, twenty-three short stories, two novels, and thirteen nonfiction pieces. The *WEDA* archive is a particularly interesting example from this period as it is representative of the fluid boundaries between print and digital. The digital archive began as a way to add materials to the print monograph. Once the archive was complete, Cole recognized that scholarly credit would not be extended to her digital work, so she published a critical article, checklist of materials, and a reprint of one short story in the journal *Legacy*. Cole's use of the digital as a means of increasing access to "lost" works is indicative of the period where the digital was seen as a tool for extending the canon.

As we moved out of the 1990s, the flurry of digital recovery projects and the promise of activist work to restructure the canon began to fade. Digital recovery projects had made a huge impact on the texts available online, but such work seemed to contrast with the growing professionalization of digital literary studies. While digital editions and archives had coexisted with digital recovery work in this earlier period, the increasing institutionalization of digital humanities shifted the focus away from such technologically simplistic work and toward more robust and complex projects. The decline of digital recovery projects will produce what Kenneth Price calls a "newly emerging digital canon of American literature." Unfortunately, the canon we now have was created "partly by design and partly by chance,"[32] a canon much more narrow than that of the contemporary print canon.

The late 2000s marked a period of rapid decline in recovery work. By 2008, most of the etext centers including the Oxford Text Archive, the UVA Etext Center, CETH, and the Carnegie Mellon center had been shuttered or absorbed by their institutions' libraries, resulting in a rapid decrease of new digital recovery projects.[33] The proliferation of early activist projects by scholars interested in recovery dropped precipitately as literary scholarship shifted its focus away from canonicity (see fig. 3.5).

JSTOR data provides a snapshot of the larger literary field's interest in particular subjects. Collecting data from journals, books, and primary sources, JSTOR data provides one context for understanding trends in scholarship. An analysis of JSTOR data from 1950 to 2014 reveals that scholarship focused on canon concerns peaked in 1999 and has been declining since that period.[34] It is not surprising that the same pattern of interest and decline is apparent in the digital record of textual recovery.

Publication Year

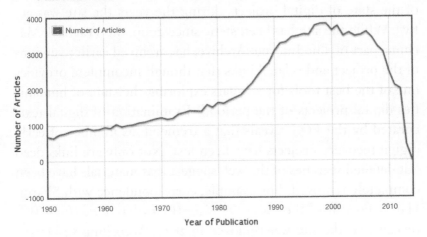

Fig. 3.5. JSTOR data, canon keyword search. Note that journal publications focused on canon peak in the late 1990s and drop through the current decade.

In addition to a decrease in new projects, a large number of digital recovery projects produced during the heyday of such work have been or are in danger of being lost, of grave concern as it is possible that we are creating a digital canon that is more representative of the literary canon of 1950 than that of the literary canon of 2014. Analysis of Alan Liu's *Voice of the Shuttle* (*VOS*), a curated hyperlinked project that compiled a broad range of primary and secondary humanities materials from 1994 to 2009, provides a means of measuring the loss of early digital recovery projects. Subjects range from the technology of writing, politics and government, photography, dance, anthropology, and cultural studies among other categories. Links to primary texts are included in multiple categories, including Literature (in English), Literatures (Other than English), Minority Studies, Cultural Studies, and Gender and Sexuality Studies. Because Liu designed the *VOS* as comprehensive and also relied on an early form of crowd sourcing, a network of scholars that contributed links and updates, the site provides an excellent measure of the state of digital projects during the years the site was active. While the site has been static since 2009, the Wayback Machine, part of The Internet Archive, has archived earlier versions of the project and related links that though incomplete provides one of the best tools for scholars exploring the state of humanities digital projects of the period.[35] Examination of digital texts curated by the *VOS* reveals that a tremendous number of early digital recovery projects have been lost. Not only are links dead but detailed searches of the web suggest that materials have been completely removed. For example, correspondence with Sharon Harris, creator of the *Early American Women's Website* (*EAWW*), reveals that the site was removed in 2011. According to Harris, there are no available backup files.[36] The loss of the *EAWW* is a familiar occurrence. Examination of projects included in the *VOS* reveals a great deal of loss. For example, contemporary writer Maya Angelou is included in the Contemporary American Authors and African American Literature categories with a total of seven sites related to her work. Only two of the seven projects remain online. Of the five original projects, we are left with scant details that we might use to locate the original documents, such as original URL, author, site creator, and hosting university. This unfortunate loss is replicated time and time again, leaving the digital literary canon smaller with each loss.

Tracking the production and subsequent loss of recovery projects reveals the haphazard history of the preservation of such projects. *The Winnifred Eaton Digital Archive* is one such example. Hosted by the University of Virginia's Etext Center as a separate and distinct digital archive from 2003 to 2010, the archive has been absorbed into the library's digital collections by the department of Digital Curation Services at the University of Virginia, and, as part of the transition, most Etext Center materials have been cleaned and migrated to stable repositories.[37] All Eaton texts, then, are preserved and available through a standard search of

VIRGO, the University of Virginia Library database. The preservation of individual recovery texts is rare and those involved in such work at the University of Virginia show great forethought. However, preservation decisions have created a new form, perhaps a new edition, of Eaton's work rather than a copy of the original archive. UVA has broken the original digital archive into individual items, in effect mimicking the original print versions of Eaton's work. In addition, the original archive includes images from magazines that accompanied the texts. These images are no longer available in the VIRGO versions.[38] Also removed from the current Eaton texts are files that include information regarding the production of the digital version of the text, such as original creator of the materials, conversion metadata, and editing history.[39] The elimination of such material erases the bibliographical markers of production that scholars are interested in viewing when they evaluate the reliability of a text. Such losses are exacerbated by the dissolution of the archive itself. The stand-alone digital archive of Eaton's works reveals the volume and breadth of her writing and gives weight to the importance of resituating Eaton within the American literary tradition. The transfer of the body of work into single entries obscures the largess of Eaton's work, and Eaton's legacy recedes into the database, leaving her recovered body of work obscured once more.[40]

The Winnifred Eaton Digital Archive is just one of many early digital recovery projects that are unstable. Some recovery projects contain texts that are unavailable as open source online materials but are found in subscription databases. Other projects have been fragmentally archived, as is the case with the Eaton materials. Still other projects have disappeared completely and are available only in the original print form from which they were recovered. All losses impact the shape of our current digital canon. Scholars spent years digitizing and recovering texts, providing open access versions of work by authors who had been understudied. Every text that has disappeared has erased crucial knowledge that will now need to be recovered or, worse, undertaken once more. The loss of a digital presence of an often reproduced canonical author may not hurt the awareness and study of the canonical author, but the loss of the single digital instance of a recovered text by a little known author will, in effect, send the author back into the hidden archives that scholars have worked to expose. Additionally, such built projects provide important cultural and historical data that reveal understandings of criticism and culture at a particular historical moment. It matters that scholars and fans chose to dedicate scholarly sites to certain authors and not others. The loss of digital recovery projects leaves gaping holes in our understanding of late twentieth-century literary scholarship. Digital humanists are fond of talking about sustainability as a problem for current and future works, but it is clear that we already have sustained a good deal of loss within the broadly defined digital canon.

While a good many of the early small-scale digital projects have been displaced or lost from our current digital canon, a few have managed not only to survive but to thrive and offer models of best practices for recovery and sustainability. Projects created in connection with an institutional structure, a university or etext center, have had a much better chance of surviving, in part because institutions understand standards and preservation approaches, have a greater possibility of staff dedicated to such work, and see the projects as part of past investments of the institution and, as such, economically and intellectually important. For example, the *Victorian Women Writers Project* was launched in 1995 and quickly became known as an exemplary digital recovery project. By mid-2000, however, the project was faded. The markup was old and incomplete, search capabilities were limited, and the project looked dated. In 2010 the Indiana University Library team, headed by Michelle Dalmau, refurbished the project.[41] Texts were recoded to meet TEI P5 standards and additional materials, including "newly encoded texts and related contextual materials like critical introductions, biographical sketches, and annotations," were added. Harnessing the expertise of digital librarians at Indiana University, graduate and undergraduate students contributed to the revision.[42] The same support is usually not offered to the one-off, stand-alone DIY projects outlined at the beginning of this chapter, which suffer from their position outside the institutional structure. Other projects have found institutional support from digital organizations, such as NINES (Nineteenth-Century Scholarship Online). The project *19: Interdisciplinary Studies in the Nineteenth Century* was initially formed as a simple HTML journal. Scholars affiliated with the project participated in a 2005 NINES summer workshop during which they learned to encode their documents with the international standard of TEI/XML. Once the project was re-marked with TEI, it was brought into the NINES federated collection of nineteenth-century materials, which expanded its user base, allowed scholars to use different tools to manipulate and examine the materials, and increased the project's chance of long-term sustainability.

The attention to infrastructure is central to what might be the most successful early recovery project, the *Women Writers Project*. The project is designed "to bring texts by pre-Victorian women writers out of the archive and make them accessible to a wide audience of teachers, students, scholars, and the general reader,"[43] a goal shared by many of the early digital DIY projects. Begun in the department of English at Brown University, later moved to Computing and Information Services and, finally, the Brown library, the *WWP* has always demonstrated its connection to the mainstream of academia. The founders of the project, Susanne Woods and Stuart Curran, brought legitimacy to the project since they were known scholars in the subject area who could command respect for their work, even when that work was being disseminated through digital means. The advisory board and initial editors were or have become leaders in their respective fields. In addition, the strategic alignment of the *WWP* with a highly respected press, Oxford, and university, Brown, suggests that the effort to position the project as inside the academy not only aids legitimacy of the project but increases its ability to be sustained.[44] Cleverly tying the new with the old, Woods suggests that harnessing traditional values and approaches to scholarship aid the sustainability of the *WWP*. As Woods describes the project, "The long-term future of the *WWP*, then, lies in its position as a bridge between old ways of reading and new."[45] Infrastructures of support, then, are a necessity in digital project preservation.

Infrastructure support extends beyond institutions to individuals who work in collective communities. Active communities are the difference between preservation and loss. Curated hyperlink projects, for example, are structured to take advantage of active communities that produce webpages. As communities lose interest, projects disappear leading to the death of links, a process that eventually renders the curated hyperlink project unusable. An active and interested community, however, is incredibly powerful as demonstrated by viral archiving examples. Viral archiving is the replication of a text for use or distribution. Perhaps the most studied text preserved through viral archiving is *Aggripa (A Book of the Dead)*, a born digital art collaboration of Dennis Ashbaugh, William Gibson, and Kevin Begos Jr. Matthew Kirschenbaum and Alan Liu's exemplary work on *Aggripa* reveals that "the text of the poem as it circulates online today is not a digital copy whose bits were lifted from one of the project's diskettes, but rather the result of a manual transcription of a video cassette . . ."[46] The hackers who chose to preserve the poem were responding to the unique challenge of a software text that was designed to be unarchivable, and though we don't have an exact replica of the original poem, a surrogate for study has remained through the communities' efforts. Similar efforts include the reproduction of a poignant letter written in 1795 by Judith Cocks, a slave in Connecticut, to her master. Originally recovered by the *Early American Women Writers* website,[47] the letter was replicated in an entry on the Women of Color in Accounting Facebook page.[48] The reproduction of the letter on a nonacademic page is not uncommon; "The Marriage of Okiku-San," a short story found within the *Winnifred Eaton Digital Archive* and reprinted by *Legacy*, is preserved in various sites including a genealogy site and various Chinese and Japanese sites.[49] While viral archiving successfully preserves texts, the happenstance approach to such preservation is by no means an appropriate long-term strategy if we are interested in producing a comprehensive humanities data set.

Crucial to establishment of an inclusive set of digital literary texts is an understanding of the role of technological standards in preservation and canonization. Digital humanists are well aware of the importance of updating technologies for preservation, and successful projects such as the *Walt Whitman Archive* have made the transition from HTML, to SGML, to TEI/XML metadata structures. However, technology standards have impacted the ways that materials are utilized, leaving some digital recovery projects unused and excluded from what is developing as technological standards that are elemental to the formation of what is and is not included in the digital literary canon. Kenneth Price alludes to the centrality of technology standards in canon selection when he argues that "people ready to embrace high quality work wherever it is found hold in highest regard digital work that features a rigorous editorial process and adheres to international standards (for example, TEI/XML)."[50] The notion of technological standardization as a marker of high quality digital work provides another clue to the displacement of digital recovery texts. An MLA bibliography search includes almost one thousand digital literary projects, yet the vast majority of the small-scale, older recovery projects included by MLA are invisible in current digital literary scholarship. Glynis Carr's *The Online Archive of Nineteenth-Century U.S. Women's Writing*, active from 1997 to 2001, is one such project listed in the MLA bibliography. A number of the texts included on the site, such as *Aunt*

Lindy by former slave Victoria Earle Matthews, are not available in digital form elsewhere. Though Matthews's text would be very useful for those examining nineteenth-century issues of religion and race in postbellum America, the text is not considered part of the current digital literary studies canon in large part because of its technological infrastructure. The project shares characteristics with other dying or lost digital recovery projects. Glynis Carr produced the project with a small number of students, without a digital humanities center or library support, and published the project on her personal staff page at the university at which she is employed. Carr is also not active within the digital humanities community. All of these reasons may contribute to the lack of attention given to the site, but perhaps most damaging is that the site was produced in HTML, a form resistant to preservation strategies and noninteroperable with current datamining approaches. A common strategy in early digital recovery projects, the use of simple technologies for digital project creation, now mark projects as "low quality," a stigma that creators of the projects are well aware. Interviews with Jean Lee Cole, creator of the *Winnifred Eaton Digital Archive*; Sharon Harris, creator of the *Early American Women's Website*; and Donna Campbell, creator of *American Authors* reveal that all three scholars believe that current technological standards have stymied project preservation. Harris, for example, reports that she removed her *EAWW* project because it was "not in a sophisticated platform."[51] Cole and Campbell both view their projects as excluded from digital literary scholarship primarily due to technological approaches. Some digital scholars see the overdetermination of technology as a disturbing trend that leads to a narrow digital literature canon. Amanda Gailey and Andrew Jewell call this trend "a 'hipster ethos'" that makes "absent" "celebrations of content-rich digital humanities projects."[52] Gailey and Jewell are concerned with current production of digital editions, but the emphasis on technological standards has an equally damaging impact on the inclusion of a diverse canon.

Barriers to digital recovery projects are also found in the current ways that we theorize what is an appropriate "text" for digitization and analysis. Margaret Ezell cautions that we have not revised the way in which we understand texts and because of this elision certain texts, particularly noncanonical texts, are not being digitized. She argues that "while we increasingly have the ability to digitalize any text we please . . . editors do not please to select certain types of material and this is in part because perhaps we are not yet changing some of the basic assumptions about what an 'edition' does, or in Hunter's terms, what is 'appropriate.'"[53] Clearly the question of canon is still in flux, regardless of the belief that such concerns were resolved by the culture wars of the last century. We might also have a historical problem in the very emergence of digital humanities that contributes to the selection of materials for digitization. Martha Nell Smith contends that digital humanities developed as a space to which practitioners fled from the shifts in the profession that arose out of the cultural studies movement. In "The Human Touch: Software of the Highest Order, Revisiting Editing as Interpretation," Smith highlights the digital humanities' retreat into modes of analytics, objective approaches as "safe" alternatives to the messy fluidities found in literary studies. She notes, "It was as if these matters of objective and hard science provided an oasis for folks who did not want to clutter sharp, disciplined, methodical philosophy with considerations of the gender-, race-, and class-determined facts of life . . . Humanities computing seemed to offer a space free from all this messiness and a return to objective questions of representation."[54] If Smith is correct, then it should be no surprise that the recovery of messy lost texts has not been a priority for the field.

Additional reasons for the exclusion of particular texts are economic. Citing a number of press directors, John Willinsky points to the continued cost of scholarly publication due to the continued need for press staff.[55] As Kenneth Price has so adroitly stated, digital materials might be free for those who use the project, "But free stuff comes from somewhere, and it is rarely, if ever, free to produce."[56] Price, who has successfully guided the *Walt Whitman Archive* through numerous grant applications, emphasizes that "the creation of digital editions is expensive, and the demand for external and internal grant support always exceeds the money available. We need to reflect, then, on what gets funded and what does not and to take care not to institute an even more narrowly conceived canon than in the past."[57] NEH grants, which fund a majority of the digital literary projects, are often judged by impact and impact is most recognized by numbers of hits to the site. We know that canonical writers have a greater chance of a large following than little known writers. So, it follows that a good number of the archive and edition projects are focused on canonical writers, such as Rossetti, Melville, or Whitman. "What is marketable in terms of digitalization projects are . . . editorial projects covering great vast expanses of materials of varying natures," states Margaret Ezell, "and that digitalization in this instances 'sells' because of its ability to include 'everything' and link it in a comprehensible searchable and sustainable system." This system tends to exclude outlying texts, including the "single, uniquely existing manuscript."[58] Such structural concerns need to remain at the fore of our work with digitization, since without careful attention to issues of the canon, we risk creating a digital canon that looks more like a New Critical canon than a contemporary, diverse body of literature.

What I am arguing seems to move against current digital humanities trends regarding preservation. As Kathleen Fitzpatrick and Matthew Kirschenbaum, among others, have argued, digital forms are far more stable than most critics presume. Forensic computing is able to recover data etched on hard drives and viral preservation has preserved games, texts like *Aggripa*, and even some of the recovered texts this chapter has reviewed. However, viral preservation or even planned obsolescence are not appropriate for certain kinds of materials, such as recovered texts. While we might bemoan the loss of Bethany Nowviskie's early digital project, *The John Keats Hypermedia Archive*, we can easily access Keats materials in print or even online.[59] The majority of the early digital recovery work discussed in this chapter, however, is not easily accessible. Few of these texts are in print. A few more are available on for-profit databases or on microfilm, but most are available only with a return to the one or two libraries that own the original physical copy of the book, journal, or newspaper. The targeted preservation of such materials is not technical, as Matthew Kirschenbaum has taught us, but social, and as a field we need to put such materials at the front of the preservation queue.

Central to our efforts is the need to build a community invested in the consideration of the digital literary canon. We need an initial targeted triage focused on digital recovery projects that reproduce materials not accessible in print or open access digital form. Successful models exist. We eventually need a thoughtful, targeted approach to recovery and preservation, but until we have resolved the larger digital preservation problem we might think in short-term increments. In "The Future of Preserving the Past," Dan Cohen writes, "Worrying too much about the long-term fate of digital materials in many ways puts the cart ahead of the horse . . . Instead of worrying about long-term preservation, most of us should focus on acquiring the materials in jeopardy in the first place and on shorter-term preservation horizons, 5 to 10 years, through well-known and effective techniques such as frequent backups stored in multiple locations and transferring files regularly to new storage media, such as from aging floppy discs to DVD-ROMs. If we do not have the artifacts to begin with, we will never be able to transfer them to one of the more permanent digital archives being created by the technologists."[60] Cohen's suggested approach won't resolve our preservation problems, but he reminds us that simple, short-term solutions might provide a stopgap measure for the hemorrhaging of recovery projects.

Existing organizations, including digital humanities centers, collectives, and existing projects, have preserved recovery projects. For example, the University of Nebraska's Center for Digital Research has provided support to projects that otherwise might have disappeared, such as Marta Werner's *Radical Scatters*. NINES and its sister organizations under the Advanced Resource Consortium (ARC) have established networks that foster and support various forms of digital work including recovery. Another avenue for increasing preservation is to incorporate legacy projects into current digital projects. Given the collaborative, extensible, interoperable nature of digital work, there is no reason why contemporary projects might not be connected to legacy projects. In effect, communities of interest are best able to engage with discussions of and experiments to preserve crucial early digital recovery texts. The communities of interest must also engage in the shifting technological and economic requirements of digital text recovery. Consortiums might be built to target the quickly disappearing early digital recovery projects. Infrastructures might be proposed to preserve instances of the various projects. Such approaches are best built into existing societies or organizations, particularly those organizations with an activist bent. For example, the College Language Association has long focused on African diaspora texts. Should the organization choose to act as a hub for recovery and preservation efforts, the effort would serve as an extension of work already underway.

One of the powerful things about the early period of digital literary studies is the DIY approach that many scholars embraced, the sheer joy and freedom of bringing important texts to the larger scholarly community. As we move from simple HTML sites to TEI and visualization projects, as we move from individual or small collective projects to larger team projects, from nonbudgeted projects to large, externally funded projects, we see fewer scholars working with digital textual recovery. This should concern digital humanists, and we should, accordingly, begin to strategize how we might reverse this trend. Small steps are underway. We need to examine the canon that we, as digital humanists, are constructing, a canon that skews toward traditional texts and excludes crucial work by women, people of color, and the GLBTQ community. We need to reinvigorate the spirit of previous scholars who believed that textual recovery was crucial to their work, who saw the digital as a way to enact changes in the canon. If, as Jerome McGann suggests, "the entirety of our cultural inheritance will be transformed and reedited in digital forms,"[61] then we must ensure that our representation of culture does not exclude work by those writers previously excluded.

CHAPTER 4

Data and the Fragmented Text

Tools, Visualization, and Datamining
or Is Bigger Better?

Personally, I think Digital Humanities is about building things. I'm willing to entertain highly expansive definitions of what it means to build something. I also think the discipline includes and should include people who theorize about building, people who design so that others might build, and those who supervise building (the coding question is, for me, a canard, insofar as many people build without knowing how to program). I'd even include people who are working to rebuild systems like our present, irretrievably broken system of scholarly publishing. But if you are not making anything, you are not—in my less-than-three-minute opinion—a digital humanist. You might be something else that is good and worthy—maybe you're a scholar of new media, or maybe a game theorist, or maybe a classicist with a blog (the latter being very good thing indeed)—but if you aren't building, you are not engaged in the "methodologization" of the humanities, which, to me, is the hallmark of the discipline that was already decades old when I came to it.

> —Stephen Ramsay, "Who's In and Who's Out," History
> and Future of Digital Humanities Panel, MLA, 2011

The first chapters of this book trace the literary approaches—textual studies, new historicism, and cultural criticism—that underlie contemporary digital literary scholarship. Sharing a theoretical terrain with traditional literary scholarship, the digital work I have traced in the first part of this book has been largely representational, with technology primarily used to create idealized or better versions than would be possible in print. Current trends in digital literary studies, and the larger digital humanities, appear to be moving away from representational concerns and toward interpretive functions as contemporary digital scholars, such as Stephen Ramsay, Franco Moretti, Matthew Jockers, Geoffrey Rockwell, and others, are using technology to devolve, manipulate, and reform the literary text. Arguing that earlier digital literary studies materials "seldom are . . . transformed algorithmically as a means of gaining entry to the deliberately and self-consciously subjective act of critical interpretation," these critics want to move the practice beyond what Ramsay calls "fact-checking" and instead employ technology to "assist the critic in the unfolding of interpretive possibilities."[1] Though Matthew Jockers views computational textual analysis as "the foundation of digital humanities and its deepest root,"[2] digital literary studies has largely ignored computational approaches until recently. If the preceding years of digital literary studies have been marked by continuity with traditional methodologies and practices, current work signals a potential break from the past. Scholarly analysis is being altered by algorithmic approaches that are beginning to produce evidence that might answer the long-standing digital humanities claim of presenting new findings through technological interventions, what might be called technological interpretation or algorithmic interpretation.[3] By focusing on tool development, visualization, and datamining, three crucial subareas of the interpretive bent of digital studies, this chapter will unravel how digital literary studies is beginning to shift from representation to interpretation.

Challenges to representational applications of technology began in digital literary studies in the early 2000s. In his 2001 volume, *Radiant Textuality*, Jerome McGann condemned the

primary methodologies of digital scholarship, "methods of sort-
ing, accessing, and disseminating large bodies of materials, and
on certain specialized problems in computational stylistics and
linguistics," and issued a prophetic challenge: "*the general field
of humanities education and scholarship will not take the use of digital technology seriously until one demonstrates how its tools improve
the ways we explore and explain aesthetic works—until, that is, they
expand our interpretational procedures.*"[4] McGann's University of
Virginia compatriot, John Unsworth, would expand McGann's
call for interpretation when, in 2003, he challenged scholars to
"demonstrate the usefulness of all the stuff we have digitized over
the last decade and more—and usefulness not just in the form of
increased access, but specifically, in what we can do with the stuff
once we get it: what new questions we could ask, what old ones
we could answer."[5] Unsworth's phrase "what new questions we
might ask" became the mantra of a subsection of the field, largely
driven by tool production as the means by which scholars might
answer Unsworth's charge, ushering in what Ramsay calls an "age
of tools." At the 2006 MLA meeting, Stephen Ramsay[6] summed
up the tools movement:

> Over the last twenty years, we have spent millions digitiz-
> ing texts and putting them online. The resulting digital
> full-text archives are among the greatest achievements in
> digital humanities. Yet for all their wonder, they remain
> committed to a vision of digital textuality firmly ensconced
> within the metaphor of the physical library. You can browse
> the text, read the text, search the text, and even download
> the text, but you can't really do much beyond that. It is time
> to start thinking of ways to exploit this data with analyti-
> cal tools and visualizations. Ideally, such tools should be an
> integral part of the experience of working with Web-based
> text collections.[7]

The emphasis on interpretive tools gained momentum and tool development and use became a focal point of digital literary studies.

As interest in tools grew, scholars began to realize that matching technology to use was central to an expansion of technological interpretation. The 2005 Summit on Digital Tools for the Humanities issued a report that, while largely speculative, identified the key concepts of interpretation, exploration of resources, collaboration, and visualization of time, space, and uncertainty that remain central to technological interpretation. Recognizing that "the use of digital tools in the humanities is, for the most part, still in its infancy," the report calls for development "of strategies to aid scholars in the use or re-use of existing tools" rather than "the creation of wholly new tools that are specially designed for the humanities."[8] The report was responding to the tension between what John Bradley views as two categories of tool use: those tools "developed specifically to support humanities scholarship" and those "not developed by humanists" but "proven . . . to be powerful tools when applied to scholarly tasks."[9] Scholars interested in constructing tools to support digital work quickly found that tool development was expensive and difficult and often led to highly idiosyncratic, nonextensible, and unsustainable tools.[10] Tools would be developed that were effective in a particular project but were not interoperable with other digital texts. For example, Collex, the collection and exhibit builder tool developed to work with the NINES dataset, is a robust tool but difficult to extend to other projects, requiring customization of the database. Other tools, such as Wordhoard and Protovis, are no longer updated, leading to possible problems. Other projects, such as MONK, were given limited funding and are ultimately less useful than experimental. Each of these problems contributes to the creation of humanities software with high experimental impact but low long-term value. For this reason, the summit encouraged scholars to find ways of using extensible tools rather than creating idiosyncratic tools. To do so, though, attention to disciplinary purpose must be central. Johanna Drucker cautions digital humanities scholars that "[t]he cultural authority of digital technology is still claimed by the fields that design the platforms and protocols on which we work."[11] Arguing that tools that represent place and space are resistant to humanities' approaches, Drucker maintains that "[f]lexible metrics, variable, discontinuous, and multi-dimensional will be necessary to realize a humanistic system for the graphical analysis of temporal relations."[12] The various problems raised by tool development are to be expected in this early, exploratory period. As the summit report notes, "When information technology is introduced into a discipline or some social activity there seem to be two stages. First, the technology is used to automate what users were already doing, but now doing it better, faster and possibly cheaper. In the second stage (which does not always occur), a revolution takes place."[13] We appear to be moving out of the first stage of technology automation to the proposed revolutionary shift in disciplinary practice. As we move into new uses of technology, however, Drucker's call for theoretical engagement with technology must remain central.

Tool development may be de rigueur in digital literary studies, but the purpose of such tool development tends to fall into two categories: representational and interpretative. Tools constructed for seemingly similar purposes, like the Versioning Machine and JUXTA, reveal crucial theoretical differences that mirror the tension between representation and interpretation. Launched at the ALLC/ACH conference in 2002, Susan Schreibman's Versioning Machine (VM) "was conceived as an exploration into how the computer as a medium and as a tool can represent text that exists in multiple versions."[14] Designed to display multiple versions of TEI/XML encoded texts, the VM is a tool to make digital editing easier (see fig. 4.1).

The tool allows the display of complicated TEI/XML docu-

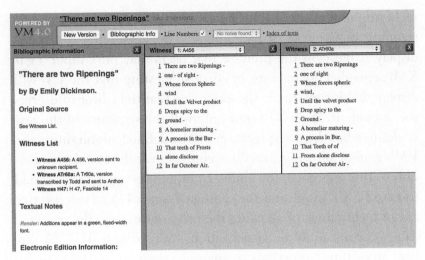

Fig. 4.1. Versioning Machine

ments that feature parallel segmentation for greater ease of editing, making the VM a tool of great use to the production of the complicated digital editions highlighted in chapter 2. The Versioning Machine is knowingly representative and holistic "unlike, for example, other electronic display paradigms such as TextArc or TagClouds, whose goal is to provide new ways of visualising the text through deformance by removing words from their syntactic contexts."[15] Designed to represent a simulacrum of a text for analysis by a scholar, rather than to probe for meaning through technological intervention, the VM has the primary goal of allowing the user to more easily edit texts. JUXTA, on the other hand, is constructed to resist representation as it is focused on "procedures of interpretative deformation."[16] Like the Versioning Machine, JUXTA compares versions of texts and allows scholars to to complete various tasks related to digital edition building including TEI/XML encoding.[17] Unlike the Versioning Machine, JUXTA is designed to work with a broader set of document forms, XML, HTML, DOC, RTF, PDF, and PUB. The decision to allow the user to input multiple format types,

including unformatted RTF files, signals a very different understanding of the role of technology. The Versioning Machine's
display is built on the premise that users may only input TEI/
XML encoded documents, in effect suggesting that the VM will
display the documents in the exact way that the editor interprets
the document. With TEI, not only will the structure of the text
be defined but the interpretation will be defined, highlighting the
VM's goal of allowing the editor control over the text. In opposi-
tion to this approach, the ability to input less rigorously defined
texts to JUXTA indicates the ceding of control to an interpretive
use of technology, of allowing the program to turn the text into
data to create multiple visualizations. Accordingly, JUXTA uti-
lizes algorithmic functions to analyze, compare, and display the
text in various ways including heat maps, side-by-side comparisons, and histograms (see figs. 4.2–4.4).

The tool is designed to create "interpretive comparisons" that
the user might then examine to fulfill "the basic humanities interpretive act: critical comparison."[18] The imagistic understanding
of textual difference, the histogram graphs and heat maps, are
built by carving the texts into discreet data points and then displaying the points in a form that the user must then rebuild into a
pattern. While both programs might be used to successfully edit
a text, the use of technology and the theoretical understanding of
a text remain crucially different in the tools.

As tool use gained momentum and interpretive possibilities
were revealed, digital humanities scholars began to argue that
tool development, or building, might be understood as an intellectual act, an argument. Foremost in the calls for such an approach has been Stephen Ramsay, who set off a firestorm when he
announced at the 2011 MLA: "If you're not making anything . . .
you're not a digital humanist." The value of building, according
to Ramsay, is interpretive by nature:

DH-ers insist—again and again—that this process of creation yields insights that are difficult to acquire otherwise.

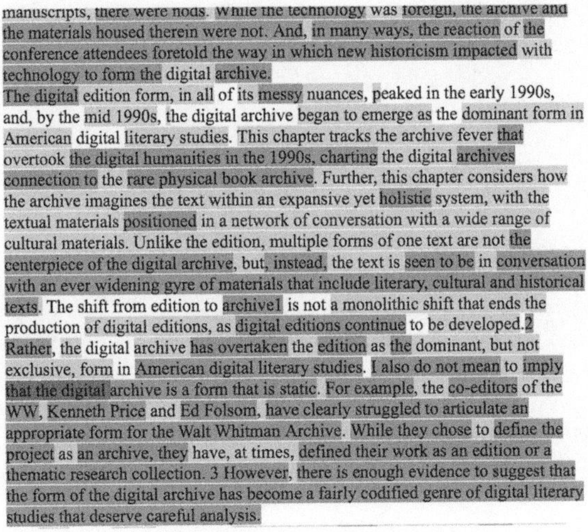

manuscripts, there were nods. While the technology was foreign, the archive and the materials housed therein were not. And, in many ways, the reaction of the conference attendees foretold the way in which new historicism impacted with technology to form the digital archive.
The digital edition form, in all of its messy nuances, peaked in the early 1990s, and, by the mid 1990s, the digital archive began to emerge as the dominant form in American digital literary studies. This chapter tracks the archive fever that overtook the digital humanities in the 1990s, charting the digital archives connection to the rare physical book archive. Further, this chapter considers how the archive imagines the text within an expansive yet holistic system, with the textual materials positioned in a network of conversation with a wide range of cultural materials. Unlike the edition, multiple forms of one text are not the centerpiece of the digital archive, but, instead, the text is seen to be in conversation with an ever widening gyre of materials that include literary, cultural and historical texts. The shift from edition to archive1 is not a monolithic shift that ends the production of digital editions, as digital editions continue to be developed.2 Rather, the digital archive has overtaken the edition as the dominant, but not exclusive, form in American digital literary studies. I also do not mean to imply that the digital archive is a form that is static. For example, the co-editors of the WW, Kenneth Price and Ed Folsom, have clearly struggled to articulate an appropriate form for the chose with the Walt Whitman Archive. While they chose to define the project as an archive, they have, at times, defined their work as an edition or a thematic research collection. 3 However, there is enough evidence to suggest that the form of the digital archive has become a fairly codified genre of digital literary studies that deserve careful analysis.

Fig. 4.2. Heat Maps

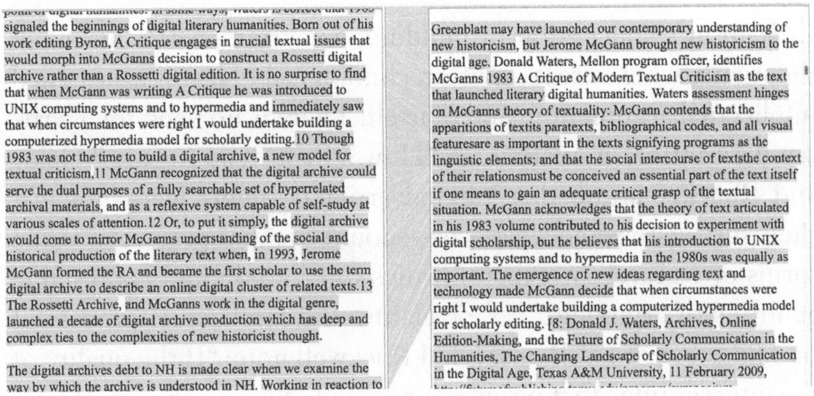

point of digital humanities. In some ways, Waters is correct that 1983 signaled the beginnings of digital literary humanities. Born out of his work editing Byron, A Critique engages in crucial textual issues that would morph into McGanns decision to construct a Rossetti digital archive rather than a Rossetti digital edition. It is no surprise to find that when McGann was writing A Critique he was introduced to UNIX computing systems and to hypermedia and immediately saw that when circumstances were right I would undertake building a computerized hypermedia model for scholarly editing.10 Though 1983 was not the time to build a digital archive, a new model for textual criticism,11 McGann recognized that the digital archive could serve the dual purposes of a fully searchable set of hyperrelated archival materials, and as a reflexive system capable of self-study at various scales of attention.12 Or, to put it simply, the digital archive would come to mirror McGanns understanding of the social and historical production of the literary text when, in 1993, Jerome McGann formed the RA and became the first scholar to use the term digital archive to describe an online digital cluster of related texts.13 The Rossetti Archive, and McGanns work in the digital genre, launched a decade of digital archive production which has deep and complex ties to the complexities of new historicist thought.

The digital archives debt to NH is made clear when we examine the way by which the archive is understood in NH. Working in reaction to

Greenblatt may have launched our contemporary understanding of new historicism, but Jerome McGann brought new historicism to the digital age. Donald Waters, Mellon program officer, identifies McGanns 1983 A Critique of Modern Textual Criticism as the text that launched literary digital humanities. Waters assessment hinges on McGanns theory of textuality: McGann contends that the apparitions of textits paratexts, bibliographical codes, and all visual featuresare as important in the texts signifying programs as the linguistic elements; and that the social intercourse of textsthe context of their relationsmust be conceived an essential part of the text itself if one means to gain an adequate critical grasp of the textual situation. McGann acknowledges that the theory of text articulated in his 1983 volume contributed to his decision to experiment with digital scholarship, but he believes that his introduction to UNIX computing systems and to hypermedia in the 1980s was equally as important. The emergence of new ideas regarding text and technology made McGann decide that when circumstances were right I would undertake building a computerized hypermedia model for scholarly editing. [8: Donald J. Waters, Archives, Online Edition-Making, and the Future of Scholarly Communication in the Humanities, The Changing Landscape of Scholarly Communication in the Digital Age, Texas A&M University, 11 February 2009,

Fig. 4.3. Side-by-Side Comparison

It's the thing I've been hearing for as I long as I've been in this. People who *mark up* texts say it, as do those who *build* software, *hack* social networks, *create* visualizations, and pursue the dozens of other forms of haptic engagement that bring DH-ers to the same table. Building is, for us, a new kind of hermeneutic—one that is quite a bit more radical than taking the traditional methods of humanistic inquiry and applying them to digital objects.[19]

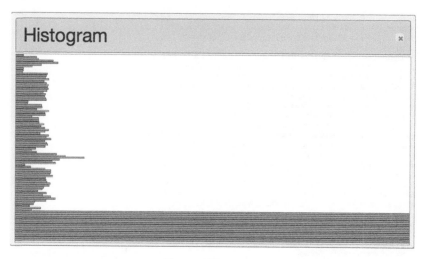

Fig. 4.4. Histogram

In Ramsay's conception of building, construction is a means of theorizing where creation of a technological object is a sustained intellectual argument in and of itself. There is no need for a written description or analysis. In "How a Prototype Argues," Galey and Ruecker argue that "digital artifacts themselves—not just their surrogate project reports—should stand as peer-reviewable forms of research, worthy of professional credit and contestable as forms of argument."[20] Correlating the intellectual process of building to writing, Ramsay and Rockwell note: "If the quality of the interventions that occur as a result of building are as interesting as those that are typically established through writing, then that activity is, for all intents and purposes, scholarship."[21] The idea of tools as stand-alone artifacts representative of scholarly intent has met significant resistance in large part because the idea displaces the written analysis as the gold standard of scholarship. Stefan Sinclair states, "The tools banish the text, that with which the literary critic is most familiar. Even tools that offer functions to view the immediate context of words can hardly be satisfying: Snippets of a text are tethered out in arbitrary chunks usually defined by character or word counts rather than natural textual boundaries such as paragraphs."[22] The replacement of the holistic text imbued with a materiality that represents the physical object with a fragmented object of study, in effect a concerted effort to break a text into discrete data points as is the case with, say, JUXTA, is a centerpiece of the digital as interpretation and what is often viewed as a direct challenge to traditional literary practice.

Most nondigital literary scholars are resistant to viewing tools as theoretically constructed arguments, seeing such an understanding of tools as antithetical to humanistic inquiry. When I ran a group session on data at the NEH sponsored NINES workshop on Evaluating Digital Scholarship, I asked participants if it was possible to assess tools as discrete scholarly artifacts. Most participants were uncomfortable with such an approach and instead argued that an article that discussed the results of the technological intervention was the only form of scholarship that might be evaluated. This is not an unsurprising response and one that has deep roots in disciplinary practice. Literary scholars are not trained to use algorithms nor to construct and apply tools to literary texts. Data representation and analysis is more closely associated with science and engineering within the specialized culture of academia than with literary analysis, and resistance to such work often arises out of tension between science and the humanities, a la C. P. Snow. As university funding and prestige is increasingly seen to correlate with STEM areas rather than humanities fields, humanities scholars have become increasingly suspect of what appear to be scientific approaches encroaching on traditional humanistic studies. As Stephen Ramsay remarks, "When we introduce computers into the field of interpretation, we bring along the inheritance of a popular conception that has always associated computers with the inexorable calculus of fact and truth."[23] As I have discussed earlier in this book, applied work, such as edition production, is not highly valued in contemporary literary studies. Tool development and use is often seen as application, and scholarship utilizing such approaches is seen as producing mechanized and simplistic treatments of complex cultural productions. The shift to recognizing building as a complement to traditional theoretical concerns is discomforting to many scholars, with scholars voicing apprehensions "that the methodology might overwhelm the humanities content, might, in fact, become the content."[24] The concern that technology or tool might become a primary object of study, displacing the literary text, threatens the centrality of long-held beliefs in the humanities. If we are to validate tool use we must, as Ramsay makes clear, provide "active resistance against the perception that we are out to provide scientific solutions to interpretive problems."[25] To do so necessitates careful interrogation of structures of technological intervention. Christine Borman stresses that "humanities scholars need to be particularly attentive to unstated assumptions about their data, sources of evidence, and epistemology. We are only beginning to understand what constitute data in the humanities, let alone how data differ from scholar to scholar and from author to reader."[26] Should we treat "data as a matter of disciplines," full of interpretive possibilities, then we might engage with what Gitelman and Jackson term "the imagination of data."[27] If we do not engage with an investigation of data within an interpretive framework, then we will have ceded meaning making to other disciplines and incompletely understood how to pair technology with use.

Another important area of growth in interpretive analysis is visualization. Visualization of texts is not new to the humanities. Instances abound in print work, according to Geoffrey Rockwell, with examples including 1970s pictorial concordances, OED project visualizations, and texts that include plots and graphs, such as Bordeiu's *Homo academicus*.[28] Current digital efforts, wordhoard, nora, TextArc, Monk, Tapor, Voyant (Voyeur), and Hyperpo, focus on "patterns in data—dynamic graphs, charts, maps, plots, etc."[29] Unlike early models, which, in the most liberal sense, are representations *of* scholarly interpretations, current experiments in visualization are representations *for* scholarly interpretation. The MONK (Metadata Offer New Knowledge) project, led by John Unsworth and Martin Mueller, is an experimental project that allows scholars to explore patterns in texts that will "produce new knowledge by exposing unanticipated similarities or differences, clustering or dispersal, co-occurrence and trends."[30] MONK provides "scientific visualizations, where numeric data about the collections are presented in visual forms, and humanities visualizations, where text data are presented in visual ways that may or may not include typography."[31] Various visualizations produced by MONK include dialR, Repetition Graph, and Walls of Text. Each of these tools is premised on the idea that the computer is able to make interpretive interventions into a text based on the scholarly team's expression of repetition through an algorithm. Put simply, the MONK team constructs an argument about word repetition, expresses that argument through an algorithm, and develops visualization tools that display the output of the algorithmic run for scholarly interpretation. MONK results are premised on a fragmented notion of text, a conversion of the seemingly whole text into data. However, the developers emphasize that while the materials are treated algorithmically as discrete datum, the tool's purpose is equally invested in context: "Shuttling between the 'micro' and the 'macro' is a distinctive feature of the MONK environment, where you may read as closely as you wish but can also practice many forms of what Franco Moretti has provocatively called 'distant reading.'"[32] Distant reading is a response to concerns that scholars have analyzed only a "minimal fraction of the literary field": "a canon of two hundred novels, for instance, sounds very large for nineteenth-century Britain (and is much larger than the current one), but is still less than one per cent of the novels that were actually published: twenty

thousand, thirty, more, no one really knows—and close reading won't help here, a novel a day every day of the year would
take a century or so."[33] To Moretti: "distance is however not an
obstacle, but *a specific form of knowledge*: fewer elements, hence
a sharper sense of their overall interconnection. Shapes, relations, structures. Forms. Models."[34] Moretti's insistence on
macro analysis raises the specter of mechanization for some critics. For Katie Trumpener, Moretti "shows statistical analysis as
a relatively blunt hermeneutic instrument, redeemed mainly by
Moretti's own exegetical verve."[35] Trumpener goes on to argue
that Moretti's brilliant close readings are actually what make his
distance readings work. Such fetishization of close reading, what
Jane Gallop calls "the most valuable thing English ever had to
offer" and "the thing that made up a discipline, that transformed
us from cultured gentlemen into a profession," has, it seems, led
some to view data-driven approaches to textual interpretation
with horror.[36] However, Moretti himself rejects the positioning
of distance reading as oppositional to close reading: "quantitative series, for their part, allow us to see new problems, whose
solution is usually found at the level of formal choices (linguistic,
rhetorical, or a mix thereof). The specific relationship between
literary form and nonliterary model varies from case to case; but
the relationship is always there."[37] By viewing close and distance
reading as approaches that are fluidly selected by the critic for
particular forms of criticism or in response to the dataset formation, Moretti's technique offers an answer to Unsworth's charge
of using technology to locate new questions. Instead of viewing
the two approaches as binary, the techniques might be seen as
selectively applicable. Timothy Burke agrees that one approach
does not preclude the use of another:

> You could still easily argue that a cultural form which oc-
> cupied a miniscule slice of the total cultural activity in a
> given era was nevertheless the most powerful, influential or

hegemonic cultural form in that time or place, or that it was the key or linchpin of popular culture in that era. You can still say that certain kinds of exemplary or highly particular works somehow best represent the spirit of a particular culture, or best problematize some of its characteristic internal struggles and contradictions. You can still do close reading of a single text (as either a historian or a literary critic) and find it valuable. But both cultural history and historicist literary criticism could benefit enormously from a truly systematic, carefully quantified account of the totality of cultural work in any given moment and place.[38]

Shifting micro and macro level readings are an attempt to balance two compelling forms of textual analysis: the traditional close reading of literary scholarship and new forms of computer driven interpretation examining patterns in a larger body of work.

MONK, then, treats texts as data for manipulation purposes but, at the same time, provides an illusion of textual wholeness, of the ability to contextualize within the larger cohesive model. The emphasis on situating individual repetitions within the larger context is crucial to the success of the project. For example, the following repetition graph displays individual data points in ways that seem to reject a textual cohesion familiar to literary scholars (see figs. 4.5 and 4.6).

Another repetition graph view, however, allows users to situate the individual items within a context.

MONK provides balance between individual data points and a contextualized view of the interpretive results, and the tool represents an important experimental intervention in visualizations. What remains an issue to traditional literary scholars, however, is the initial interpretive function that treats text as data points. Human interpretation of texts is not easily transferred to algorithmic functions. Simple tasks, such as "hyphenated words at the end of a line or a page" "are major stumbling blocks in work-

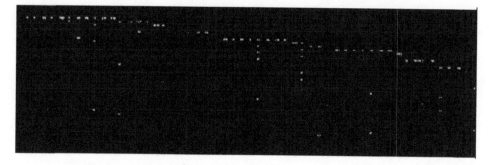

Fig. 4.5. Repetition graph, individual points. (Ruecker et al., "Visualizing Repetition in Text.")

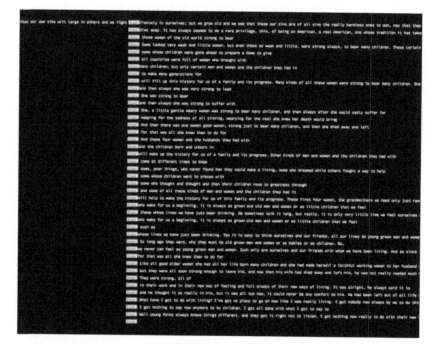

Fig. 4.6. Repetition graph, contextualized. (Ruecker et al., "Visualizing Repetition in Text.")

flows that aim at creating a document space in which texts of different origins can be treated as members of a single corpus."[39] While those involved with the creation of technological methods of interpretation recognize that such roadblocks will eventually be resolved, critics of the work see such problems as evidence of an intrinsic disconnect between humanistic interpretation and technology.

To address the resistance to our work in visualization and tool development we must focus on expanding our experimental approaches, sharing our results, and frankly discussing current limitations in the work. There are models of forward thinking experimentation, such as Tanya Clement's investigation of Gertrude Stein's *The Making of Americans*. Stein's frustrating text has long been difficult to analyze using traditional methods, with scholars claiming the text "is inchoate—the early work of an inexperienced author—and as such its constant repetition represents a style of writing that is chaotic, unsystematic, and virtually impossible to read."[40] MONK's ability to visualize repetition, a motif in Stein's work, makes it the perfect tool for use in the textual analysis, and Clement's visualizations reveal that Stein groups frequencies of repetition by chapter (see fig. 4.7).

With MONK's visualizations, Clement provides convincing evidence that the novel is carefully structured, and that the frequency groupings were structured to produce meaning, a finding antithetical to previous readings of Stein's work. Instead of viewing the text as fragmented into random pieces, "Each part is as important as the whole," a reading that is supported by the visualization. However, the literary scholar examining the article might remain unconvinced, as methodology and visualizations are partitioned from traditional scholarly analysis, reinforcing the belief in the incompatibility of algorithmic function within humanistic inquiry. This is not an entirely fair critique of the article, as the article's publication in *Literary and Linguistic Computing* means that the audience skews toward technologically advanced

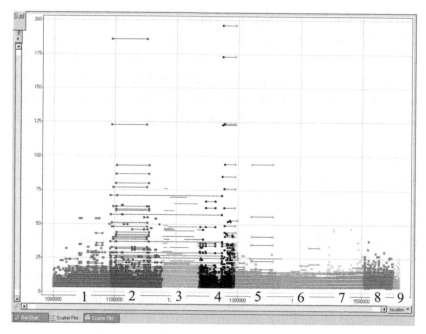

Fig. 4.7. Visualization of repetition over location (*x*-axis) and length (*y*-axis).

readers. However, scholars involved in such experimental work are challenged to integrate what is often seen as the binary of algorithmic interpretation and humanistic analysis. Accordingly, if the tool does not easily reveal the underlying assumptions and approaches that drive the algorithmic interpretation, as is the case with MONK, then greater emphasis on the humanistic interpretation must be provided by the scholar to assuage concerns of traditional humanistic scholars.

While we should applaud new readings of texts enabled by distant reading, and Clement provides one of the best now available, we must also recognize that the tool through which the reading is created is not neutral and may impact the way in which one reads the texts. Just as literary critics recognize that cultural biases might appear in their work, tool biases are also possible. This is not a problem with technology or tools. This is a deeper issue related to interpretation of all types, and rather than dismissing tools for such biases, we should, instead, recognize that tool bias might, at this moment, be more apparent than the naturalized biases in traditional literary interpretation. We must continue to critique machine-aided interpretation in the same way that we critique interpretation through traditional means; we must attend to the "human element" of not only the text but the data and the software.[41] One of the most useful ways to begin this process is to facilitate exchange between data and tool, output and analysis.

Critics that reject datamining often do so because they believe that algorithmic approaches are too generalized, simplistic, and unreflective of the complexity of human cultural artifacts. What they fail to realize is that current datamining limitations are in large part due to the poor data on which we perform algorithmic criticism. For example, Trumpener complains about the lack of cross-cultural comparatives in Moretti's work on the British book title, which Moretti says is indeed true because the British dataset was the only data available digitally for his manipulation. Laura Mandell has quipped, "we don't HAVE data yet."[42] By this, Mandell means that we don't have complete or broad sets of *accurately* digitized materials.[43] As scholars turned away from editing and early forms of digital textual representation to experimental uses of technology for interpretation, the digitization of texts by scholars declined. For-profit companies like Gale or Google seemed to be digitizing our cultural heritage materials at a rapid clip, making small-scale scholarly digitization projects less attractive and seemingly without use. Unfortunately the texts produced by such groups contain gaps in digitization and search capabilities that limit their use. Mandell notes:

> scholars believe that the "Gale Group" has taken care of
> it. Gale produced ECCO, Eighteenth-Century Collections

Online, a dataset that seemingly single-handedly solves the problem of transferring 18th-century texts to digital media. There had been a microfilm project for capturing all the eighteenth-century texts listed in a renowned bibliography in the field—all 400,000 of them. It had begun in the late 1970s, and libraries all over the Anglo-American world had participated, beginning with the British Library. Gale had taken over that microfilm collection and created digital image files out of 138,000 of the 200,000 that had been filmed. But image files aren't data. Having images online makes them easier to look at but not fundamentally different from microfilm. Leaving those texts as image files is almost as good as burying them in the backyard.[44]

Mandell's focus on the limitations of searching is also related to use. Images are not available for algorithmic criticism without translation, and the translation engines, Optical Character Recognition, or OCR, are problematic.[45] OCR quality is variable for texts, with older texts presenting font problems. The long "s" in eighteenth-century texts, for example, is often misread by the OCR engine: "So somebody could search for 'cases' and look through the results and say, 'Nobody ever sued anybody for divorce in the 18th century.' And that wouldn't be true," says Mandell.[46] Diana Kichuk agrees that conversion often produces poor data and points to the example of Early English Books Online's (EEBO) digital scans made from microfilm copies, which muddies the image capture due to the microfilm's poor quality. Add to this a good bit of "content amputation" and page distortion, and the final data becomes unreliable.[47] Google Books has similar technological problems including OCR and search limitations, well documented by critics including Geoffrey Nunberg, who has been outspoken in his critique of misnaming, misdating, and other metadata errors in Google Books. Unlike proprietary databases, such as EEBO or Eighteenth-Century Collections

Online (ECCO), there is not a scholarly selection process for what Google digitizes. Instead, Google is taking all materials found on its partners' library shelves for conversion. Although we might argue that selection occurred when librarians chose to purchase or collect these materials, in many ways Google Books remains far less constrained than products like EBBO or ECCO. Often obscure materials are available from Google Books because no one is deciding what goes in and what goes out, unlike is the case with for-profit digital datasets that are often severely distorted. A 2008 *Library Journal* review states that ECCO "includes nearly every significant English-language title and edition published between 1701 and 1800 in the UK, along with thousands of important works from the Americas—amounting to full-text searching of some 33 million pages of material."[48] The touted comprehensiveness of EBBO, and other primary datasets like it, has been called into question by scholars. First, the materials included are often incomplete due to their provenance. For example, the *Early English Books Online* (*EEBO*) draws on the *Early English Books* microfilm facsimile collection, based on the *Short Title Catalogue of English Books*. While there have been efforts to extend the *Short Title Catalogue of English Books*, the genesis of EBBO, then, is in the 1970s. This leads to a skewing of the types of materials included in the collection due to shifts in canonical inclusion. EEBO is incomplete, with estimates that it contains "80 percent of the surviving print record in English from 1475–1700."[49] If we utilize these materials for datamining, we will produce stilted results, exactly what critics of datamining charge. Instead of rejecting datamining altogether, however, we must instead be realistic about the types of data that we use for our work, making clear where limitations occur. The lack of accuracy of these datasets will necessarily be reflected in the types of results that we might produce when datamining.

Those producing experimental datamining tools need to be forthright about how limitations of datasets impact their scholarship. For example, the creators of MONK argue that, "For users of public domain materials, MONK provides quite good coverage of 19th century American fiction, downloadable as TEI P-5 files, with or without part-of-speech annotation, or available for exploration in the user interfaces developed by the MONK project."[50] Indeed, MONK does provide good coverage, but *not good enough* coverage for scholars of literature. MONK's test set of data is drawn from several databases and digital projects, including *Documenting the American South*, *Early American Fiction*, *EEBO*, *ECCO*, *19th Century Fiction*, *Shakespeare*, and *Wright American Fiction, 1850–75*. Of these, *Documenting the American South*, *Early American Fiction* and *Wright American Fiction*[51] cover American texts. In comparing the seventh edition *Norton American Literature Anthology* to the Americanist data available in MONK it is clear that the dataset is, at best, spotty. What is unexpected, perhaps, is that some later canon additions, such as Frederick Douglass, Fanny Fern, or Harriet Beecher Stowe, are available while canonical authors Emerson, Thoreau, and Jonathan Edwards are absent. There is a lack of coverage of Native American texts with now canonical writers such as Sarah Winnemucca and Zitkala Sa absent. Related materials, such as the captivity narrative of Mary Rowlandson, are also absent.[52] If we were interested in exploring representations of Native peoples in literature we would be neglecting crucial voices if we use this dataset. The issue of data inclusivity is not a problem with MONK, the tool. It is instead a systemic problem across the whole of humanities. Instead of claiming that datamining is able to definitively answer questions we must realize that we are in the infancy of algorithmic criticism. As the MONK project reveals, digital datasets "are large enough and rich enough to provide an excellent opportunity for text-mining, and we believe that web-based text-mining tools will make those collections significantly more useful, more informative, and more rewarding for research and teaching."[53] No doubt text mining will prove our datasets to be more useful, but "large enough" and "rich" enough are dependent on the types of texts under consideration and the algorithmic approach applied to the dataset. Certainly sets that exclude particular groups of writers are not good enough. At this moment datamining is unable to produce accurate findings, and to resolve this problem we must continue to expand the data we are examining. The importance of good data—complete, accurate, and interoperable—will need continual effort over the next decade.

Unfortunately in our excitement to champion the new algorithmic form we often overstate our results and downplay the issues with our datasets. For example, Matthew Wilkens has completed very interesting datamining work using the MONK tool, but problems with the dataset make his work a cautionary tale. Wilkens uses *The Wright American Fiction* dataset to examine geographical locations mentioned in American literary texts, publishing his results in his *American Literary History* article "The Geographic Imagination of Civil War-Era American Fiction."[54] While Wilkens's article addresses a very interesting problem and is potentially quite revealing, his work is an example of what happens when we do not attend to the datasets that we are using. *The Wright American Fiction* dataset was constructed by Lyle Wright in 1957 and revised in 1965. A librarian at the Huntington Library, Wright inventoried the holdings of eighteen American libraries.[55] James Harner summarizes the dataset: "A bibliography of American editions of separately published American fiction, including novels, romances, tall tales, allegories, and fictitious biographies and travels but excluding juvenile fiction, jestbooks, Indian captivity narratives, periodicals, annuals, gift books, folklore, tracts published by religious societies, dime novels, and subscription series."[56] Harner goes on to note that the dataset is "not comprehensive," with the materials excluded from the database numerous. Specific novels by African American writers, such as *Our Nig* by Harriet Wilson, are missing and large categories of serialized novels and juvenile fiction are excluded. We should also realize that American library holdings and library selection criteria would introduce bias to the dataset. The fact that this dataset was constructed prior to canon expansion in the 1970s and 1980s requires us to be careful about how we use the data. Unfortunately, these issues are not reflected in Wilkens's analysis. Wilkens writes, "There are some squarely canonical works included in this collection, including *Moby-Dick* and *House of the Seven Gables*, but the large majority are obscure novels by the likes of T. S. Arthur and Sylvanus Cobb."[57] The canonical elisions need to be considered as part of the analysis, particularly since Wilkens is drawing conclusions about canon formation. Had Wilkens maintained that his results reflected an understanding of literature formed by scholars in the new critical era, the era that formed his dataset, his findings would have been relevant. His results do not reveal, however, a truth about American literature removed from a particular historical context because the dataset is limited by its construction.

Data issues mar the effectiveness of otherwise superb tools. For example, the UC Berkley WordSeer tool analyzes grammatical strings, allows reading and annotation, heat maps, and word frequencies. WordSeer is a remarkably useful tool, but the data set used to test the tool and the conclusions drawn about the texts are problematic. The team chose to examine the slave narratives from *Documenting the American South*, an early digitization project. They ran an analysis on the set to see if the literary conventions of the text corresponded with critic James Olney's claim that autobiographical slave narratives include a set number of tropes, such as "I was born" or "Cruel slavemaster" or "barriers to literacy."[58] However, the chosen data set was not appropriate for the research question. The three hundred narratives labeled slave narratives in *Documenting the American South* are actually a mixed bag of first person narratives that are fictional and nonfictional, black authored and white authored, pre- and post-Civil War, some autobiographical, some biographical, and some anti and some pro slavery, or at least apologetic. Of the narratives that the team utilized, a few are authored without intervention, such as Frederick Douglass's 1845 *Narrative*; others are authored with a good deal of intervention, perhaps even manipulation, such as *The Confessions of Nat Turner*; others have been proven false slave narratives, such as the *Narrative of Archy Moore*; and still others are colonization religious narratives, such as the *Life of Jeduhi Ashmun*, a narrative that convinced transcendentalist Elizabeth Peabody to support the antislavery cause. Given the narratives, it is hard to believe that Olney's criteria, which he says are to be applied to black-authored autobiographies, would be possible to prove with the chosen test set. As Olney emphasizes, his criteria are indicative of a writer who is "not fictionalizing."[59] Ultimately, WordSeer cannot be used to answer the research question posed because the dataset is not up to the challenge. Here I am challenging those in the datamining community who dismiss canon as a "debate about space on the syllabus"[60] or as less about the canon of data and more about "who has access to and can manipulate the data."[61] While I take their point that we do not have anything close to an inclusive canon, even that such a thing may never be realized, I think it is a mistake to dismiss the issue as something that has been resolved or might be sidestepped if we want big data to reveal the complexities of literature. It is crucial that we carefully examine the contours of a dataset and recognize what is revealed and what is hidden. There is still great value in the small, scholarly curated data set and we shouldn't think of such work as antithetical to large-scale projects, as the limitations of our datasets make small-scale datamining approaches far more accurate than those that take on a broader scope. If we want to be able to fully realize the possible benefits of datamining we will need a renewed effort in text digitization that occurs in tandem with experimental approaches in datamining, visualization, and geospatial representations. Recent critiques have tended to separate the two, a mistake that will damage both efforts.

What datamining offers most productively at this moment is the display of gaps and anomalies. Matthew Kirschenbaum argues that where the algorithm, the visualization, or the dataset breaks down is a crucial point for scholarly engagement; "we're interested in provocation, anomaly, and outlier results as much or more than in what we think the system actually gets right."[62] Such an approach represents an exciting way to understand the potential use value of interpretive approaches to technology. Exemplary work, such as Lauren Klein's "The Image of Absence: Archival Silence, Data Visualization, and James Hemings," suggests how our experimentation with elision might offer new interpretations.[63] Klein examines the *Papers of Thomas Jefferson Digital Edition (TJDE)*, a collection of letters, books, papers, and addresses, for what the "archival silences" might reveal about James Hemings, Jefferson's enslaved cook and brother to Sally Hemings.[64] Noting the prevalence of archival silence in "the archive of the antebellum United States," and asking pertinent questions about how scholars might "identify and extract meaning from the documents in slavery's archive," Klein "demonstrates how a set of techniques that derive from the fields of computational linguistics and data visualization help render visible the archival silences implicit in our understanding of chattel slavery today."[65] A search for James Hemings's name in the *TJDE* reveals no hits, reinforcing his absence from the archive. Through careful and targeted interpretive interventions, Klein is able to reveal a great deal of information about Hemings and the social and cultural networks he existed within. Through an analysis of individual names mentioned in Jefferson's letters,[66] Klein is able to prove that "the arcs that link Jefferson to the men and women he enslaved are much more prominent than those that link him to his family members and friends, indicating the degree to which Jefferson relied on his enslaved plantation staff to implement his various directives about such matters such as the purchase of supplies or the sale of goods"[67] (see fig. 4.8).

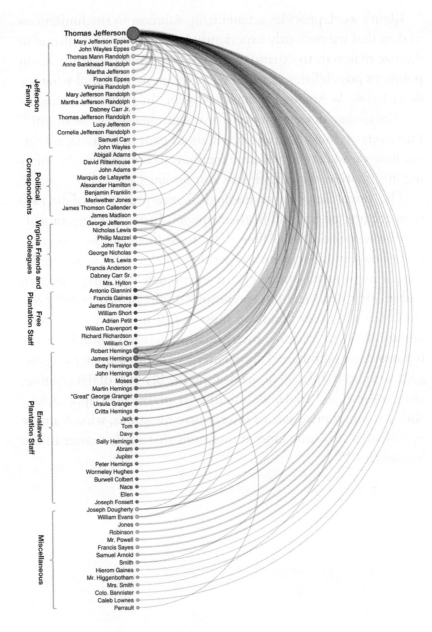

Fig. 4.8. Visualization of Jefferson's relation arcs. (Klein, 573.)

Klein's work provides a tantalizing solution to the limitations of data that we currently experience. While we must continue to digitize materials to expand our datasets for interpretation, Klein points to possibilities of using what we know to reveal what we don't know. As Amanda French insists in "In Praise of Humanities Data," data does not have to be comprehensive to be useful.[68] However, we must be transparent about gaps in datasets, revealing how we adjust our research methods to accumulate the missing information that might skew our findings.

The possibilities of technological interpretation of literary texts are myriad but still in their infancy. Instead of rejecting algorithmic approaches as flawed, we must focus on the construction of data in tandem with experimental algorithmic manipulations. Literary datasets are clearly incomplete and dirty, but even within such data new interpretations might be successfully derived. On the other hand, we must not dismiss concerns about literary data. Algorithmic interpretation depends upon both the input and the output, and digital literary studies must actively engage with both. Instead of overstating the benefits of datamining, visualization, and tools, we might best praise such approaches' ability to open materials to interpretive questions, what Ramsay rightly calls "the only kind of questions that really matter in the humanities."[69]

CHAPTER 5

Notes on the Future of
Digital Literary Studies

> As the worldview of code assumes comparable importance to
> the worldviews of speech and writing, the problematics of in-
> teraction between them grow more complex and entangled.
>
> —Katherine Hayles, *My Mother Was a Computer: Digital
> Subjects and Literary Texts*, (Chicago: U Chicago P,
> 2010), 31

The rhetoric of these statements (which could easily be
multiplied) is not one of reform, but of revolution. As Mark
Sample puts it, "It's all about innovation and disruption. The
digital humanities is really an insurgent humanities." The
project is insurgent in relation, first, to the present exclusionary structures of access and accreditation and, second, to
the hegemony of global capitalism of which those structures
are an extension. Digital humanities, declares the Manifesto,
"have a utopian core shaped by its genealogical descent from
the counterculture-cyberculture of the '60s and '70s. This is
why it affirms the value of the open, the infinite, the expansive
[and] the democratization of culture and scholarship."

> —Stanley Fish, "The Digital Humanities and the
> Transcending of Mortality," Opinionator, *The New York
> Times*, January 9, 2012

This volume is designed to explore the ways in which digital literary scholarship has developed in the last twenty years, but it
is not an answer to the perennial question "what are the digital

humanities?" Too much of the current work on digital scholarship has tried to define the field or practice within a contemporary framework, often insisting that the digital humanities are a
revolutionary force to challenge all that comes before. In reality,
the digital humanities owes a debt to a number of theoretical
strains as outlined in this volume, and its ability to alter structures, whether theoretical or institutional, is always already contained by the very infrastructure in which it currently exists, the
American academy. To argue that digital humanities are a brand
new construction seems naïve at best, destructive at worst, as it
creates an inaccurate binary that leads to increasingly hysterical
readings of the digital humanities as usurper. As I revised this
chapter, Adam Kirsch's "Technology Is Taking Over English Departments: The False Promise of the Digital Humanities" made
waves within the academic community with charges of the "obviously anti-humanistic manifestations of digital humanities."[1] As
this project reveals, various humanistic traditions, theories, and
practices do indeed construct the subfield of digital literary criticism, and the charge of antihumanism ignores a long history of
borrowing and modifying from the traditional humanities practices, from the fields of textual studies, literary criticism, and cultural criticism. In this book, I separate what Matthew Kirschenbaum calls the "*construct* of a 'digital humanities'" from the
practice of digital humanities by scholars of literature.[2] Instead of
focusing on the institutional use of digital humanities or digital
humanities as a (hopeful/destructive) political term, I am much
more interested in the work of digital humanities as it has been
and will be enacted. At the same time, this project recognizes that
the future of digital literary studies is yet unmapped and various
institutional, political, and economic forces may alter how the
field develops in yet unknown ways. To this end, the project has
focused on how current digital literary practice understands its
relationship to what has come before and what will follow.

Accordingly, this book has resisted the notion of the digital humanities as "big tent," a field or practice or theory that is broad, expansive, and inclusive, instead insisting on specificity as a counter narrative to that of the sweeping representation of revolutionary change. While some may see the segmentation of digital humanities as counterproductive, I argue that digital humanities must be particularized because DH, as enacted, is so broad, diffuse, and flexible that a generalized definition does not adequately address the various digital approaches currently in use nor how certain humanities fields are being altered by digital practice. As Tom Scheinfeldt notes, "I believe an examination of our different disciplinary histories will advance even our interdisciplinary purposes: understanding what makes us distinctive will help us better see what in our practices may be of use to our colleagues in other disciplines and to see more clearly what they have to offer us."[3] While I agree with Scheinfeldt that we do need to develop an understanding of multiple histories, I want to resist seeing multidisciplinarity as merely a catalog of items that other disciplines might offer to digital practice, as such an approach suggests cooptation and exploitation. A far more productive understanding of our collective histories is to identify the borders of practice and to look for disciplinary overlaps that benefit all partners.

Digital literary studies, as I have defined the field in this volume, is constructed from textual studies, new historicist theory, cultural studies theory, and computational applications, each of which compose the theoretical framework for our current practice. Initial digital edition production utilized book technologies to become the first visible form in digital literary studies, and digital edition production—from the recently launched *Scholarly Editing*, which features "small" editions, to the digital conversion of long-standing print editorial projects, such as the *DigitalDonne: The Online Variorum*—remains a cornerstone of contemporary scholarship. Textual studies and book history have given us theoretical structures and methodologies by which we might understand technologies of production, approaches we might borrow from print production and apply to digital production, with exemplary projects like Matthew Kirschenbaum's *Mechanisms: New Media and the Forensic Imagination* revealing the continuity between the seemingly disparate areas. At the same time, we have also inherited the unfortunate representation of textual studies as mechanistic and antitheoretical. Primarily associated with editing as an application, digital humanities insistence on more hack, less yack has been interpreted as a resistance to theoretical engagement in favor of application and left us open to charges of "DH as a *refuge* from theory."[4] Regardless of a clear tradition of theoretical engagement within textual studies and the practice of editing, some, like Richard Grusin, condemn digital humanists of creating an "invidious distinction between making things and merely critiquing them."[5] As we move forward, it is important to reveal how critiques of digital humanities as antitheoretical are misreading what are actually deep theoretical roots that are derived from textual studies.

New historicism has taught us how to situate our object of study within a social structure, whether the object of study is a computer program and its interaction with the user, a digital object within a larger network, or digital humanities within the larger context of literary studies. We might locate the digital humanist fascination with institutional power structures as a crucial legacy sprung from new historicism. As new historicists examined the complexities of power in the historical moment, current digital humanists often examine power structures within the academic institution. Unfortunately, the digital humanists' critique of institutional structures is often seen as an attack on the humanities. For example, many essays in the special issue of *differences*, "In the Shadows of the Digital Humanities," charge current digital humanists with being complicit in the growing critique against the humanities and the larger American higher educational system. David Golumbia, for example, argues that "[w]ere they more concerned with the problems of ideology and more conscious of its tenacity, DHers might see how uncomfortably close the doctrine they advocate is to many of the most extreme ideological attacks on higher education mounted the world over by the political right."[6] Grusin also asserts "that it is no coincidence that the digital humanities has emerged as 'the next big thing' at the same moment that the neoliberalization and corporatization of higher education has intensified in the first decades of the 21st century."[7] Such critiques are oddly reminiscent of charges levied against new historicism during the height of its popularity. Lee Patterson, for example, accused new historicism of "unintended conservatism."[8] Donald Pease charged new historicism with "linguistic colonialism."[9] These charges against new historicism are strangely familiar, echoing in much of the most charged condemnations of digital humanities. Walter Benn Michaels noted of anti-new historicist sentiment: "The debate over resistance and complicity is just a rerun of the old debate over the possibility of truly radical political change, a rerun made possible by the historicist appropriate of an essentially deconstructive model of political difference. Difference in deconstruction is crucially subversive, which is to say—translated to the level of culture—that differences within a culture must be understood as the difference of the culture from itself."[10] The digital humanities insistence on difference, difference in approach to scholarship, in types of methodologies, in the way that we do scholarship, is an active form of resistance to traditional academic hierarchies that many working in digital humanities find limiting. The critique of the humanities is not, as Golumbia suggests, an alignment with cyberlibertarianism but rather an attack on what many digital humanists see as academia's rigid hierarchy, the academy's insistence on practices that are, at heart, antidemocratic, antimeritocratic, and exclusionary.

Despite the increasing centrality of digital humanities to many fields and to literature in particular, digital scholars continue to insist that they retain an outsider status in large part because they want to see themselves as challenging exclusionary institutional practices. For example, blog writer bitnetted denies that DH scholars exert institutional power; "On the whole, DH people are not as structurally empowered within the academy as the theory leaders of the 80s and 90s were. That there are some senior 'names' in the field is great, but the field itself is still heterogenous [*sic*] and developing. As was pointed out in several sessions, many DH people are grad students, non TT, or staff. Those who are attempting to do such work from the TT are stressed about whether any of it will count towards T&P, especially if they are of the making or coding variety of digital humanists."[11] Lisa Spiro jokes that DHers as "in-crowd" is "an ironic label for a group of people who have long felt like misfits."[12] Others, such as Stefan Sinclair, argue that "so-called stars" are not really stars because they "are truly among the most humble and down-to-earth colleagues I can imagine. These are people who love doing their work and who spend an unbelievable amount of their time contributing altruistically to the community. These are people who volunteer huge amounts of time working behind the scenes on committees, advocating for the digital humanities at various levels, helping to provide support and expertise for other colleagues, mentoring junior colleagues formally and informally, and the list goes on."[13] The resistance to seeing digital humanists as those who have some sort of academic star quality or power in the profession has become the norm, ironic in the face of the increasing opportunities for those who are visible digital humanities scholars. Regardless of insistence by digital humanists that they are outsiders, it is abundantly clear that digital humanities has begun to exert power within traditional academic structures. Perhaps the best articulation of the way in which power and privilege works within the system comes from Kirschenbaum, who argues that while certain forms of technology can act as a "democratizer: the individual with a 4/4 load at an isolated teaching institution can wield influence in ways that would have been unthinkable in the theory-era," DH stardom and power "is not any less divorced from the real world balance of academic power, which (still) manifests in the form of jobs, grants, publications, invitations and all the rest of the apparatus."[14] We need critical attention to the fluid relationship of power structures and their relation to academic infrastructure, and we need DH scholars to be sensitive to how such power dynamics replicate privilege.

Current critiques couched as a battle between insiders and outsiders are unnuanced and potentially destructive forms of resistance to what could be productive dissent. For some, the resistance to critique comes because of what seems to be a lack of understanding about positionality. Roger Whitson, for example, says "movements like #transformDH (a group that has criticized digital humanities for its lack of attention to race, ethnicity, gender, class and sexuality) baffle me . . . if my experience with the MLA is any indication, the digital humanities doesn't need to be changed."[15] Whitson's dismissal of #transformDH's response to MLA lacks a critical positionality that replicates exclusionary practices. Much like those who continue to insist on the outsider status of DH, Whitson doesn't recognize when he slips into a position of power or at least comfort from which others might continue to be excluded. Such concerns have also turned on the specter of race that continues to overlay discussions of who is in and who is out in digital humanities in increasingly uncomfortable, problematic ways. Reverberations of race thread through digital humanities writing, including Jean Bauer's "Who You Calling Untheoretical." Written in response to Natalia Cecire's blog "When DH Was in Vogue; or, THATCamp Theory," Bauer's use of the phrase "who you calling" connects linguistically to accusations of racial impurity. As early as the nineteenth century, Southern apologist and plantation myth author Thomas Nelson Page used "Who you callin' nigger" in his work *In Ole Virginia*. Page recirculates the phrase in *Unc' Edinburg* and, throughout the nineteenth and twentieth centuries, the skewed grammatical construction was used when charging a character with racial taint. The lack of critical awareness of the problematic historical legacy invoked by the phrase is particularly poignant when we recognize that the blog is a response to Cecire's conscious play on "When the Negro was in Vogue," a Langston Hughes essay critical of whites who frequented Harlem during the jazz age to view the exotic spectacle of blackness. The connection of impurity to those interested in shifting digital humanities work to discussions of race is by no means intentional racism but a product of a long cultural use of race to represent contagion. We should not be surprised to see such a treatment of race show up within such discussions, as the American academy is, at heart, connected to deep inequities based on race and class. Instead of attacking the individuals who have utilized such analogies, we need to embrace the chance to have engaged conversations that strengthen the work that we conduct.

In fact, the embrace of cultural studies criticism and what the field has taught us about power dynamics models must be integrated into digital humanities if we truly want revolutionary shifts in academic culture. If we imagine, as Alan Liu suggests, digital humanities as a "service" "advocating the humanities in its present moment of need,"[16] then we might begin to envisage how to deconstruct power structures in the institute in which digital humanities resides, the university. In February 2010, Willard McCarty posted an analysis of a Yale graduate student conference, "The Past's Digital Presence," to the Humanist listserv. Quoting Ed Ayers, McCarty agreed that the conference might prove "a watershed event in the history of our field in the U.S."[17] McCarty's comment drew numerous responses to Humanist. Some questioned if we should celebrate such initial explorations just because they were happening at an Ivy when scholars on the ground at places like Maryland, Virginia, Nebraska, and Kentucky, among others, have been working with digital humanities for years, often at great expense to their own careers. As Amanda

Gailey eloquently argues, "I view the late arrival of the Ivies as a worrisome indicator that DH will soon be locked down by the same tired socio-economic gatekeeping mechanisms that prevent many people with talent from succeeding at so many other academic disciplines . . . [I]t is quite possible that a hitherto unproven field, within which smart people not housed at the most selective and expensive universities could actually earn influence and rewards, is becoming less egalitarian."[18] Gailey's response to the conference is one which is worth taking seriously. If DH is going to effect change, then we must continually evaluate power dynamics. If we do not, then DH will be subsumed into the larger academic culture and the revolutionary impulse will be denied.

Even detractors of digital humanities recognize that technology has already made major changes in the study of humanistic thought and production of scholarly work. Production of the objects of study is increasingly digital, and clearly the mechanisms of our scholarly output, the presses that produce, say, monographs, are already responding to technological change. While we may bring our traditional methodologies and theories to bear on technologically produced humanities materials, we will also want to respond, in the way humanists have always responded, to the shifting landscape of cultural production. Much of what we are now able to do with algorithmic interpretation has never before been possible, yet there is much experimentation yet to occur. Instead of clinging to our old methods, it seems that humanists would be best served by experimental uses of new tools to expand the humanistic inquiry in which we have long been engaged.

Because the digital humanities continue to have such a long history of interaction with and derivation from recognizable humanistic models, it is surprising that DH is often seen as threatening and antihumanistic. It seems likely that the threat posed by DH stems from the institutional, structural changes that digital humanists advocate. Kirschenbaum highlights the ways by which digital humanists work differently than traditional humanists:

". . . the digital humanities today is about a scholarship (and a pedagogy) that is publicly visible in ways to which we are generally unaccustomed, a scholarship and pedagogy that's bound up with infrastructure in ways that are deeper and more explicit than we are generally accustomed, a scholarship and pedagogy that is collaborative and depends on networks of people and that lives an active, 24/7 life online." Kirschenbaum closes his essay by asking: "Isn't that something you want in your English department?"[19] But the very issues he points to, the very issues that make DH unique within the humanities—collaboration, real time scholarship, open access, restructuring of academic hierarchies—are exactly the structural and infrastructural points of tension with traditional humanists, the point of resistance for many in English departments. For many scholars, the more public the publication, the more suspicious the scholarly rigor of the work. Public blogs are accused of being CV filler rather than seen as disseminating our work to a broader public or, worse, selling out to a neoliberal plot of assigning use value to our scholarly production. As digital humanities makes inroads into traditional departments, conferences, journals, and fields, it becomes more and more apparent that the thing that is threatening about digital humanities work is not the work itself but how digital humanists choose to work. Creation of a digital text makes sense within a disciplinary framework but working in collaborative teams to produce multi-authored scholarship is a practice far afield from how most literary scholars work.[20] My participation in the 2011–2012 NINES/NEH Summer Institute on Evaluating Digital Scholarship made clear just where the tensions in the new working structures appeared. For participants in the institute, departmental and university administrators, forms that looked like traditional forms, such as digital journals or even articles and books analyzing digital tools or approaches, were acceptable modes of scholarship. The MLA likewise agrees that an electronic journal is "a viable and credible mode of scholarly production."[21] Of far greater controversy are the types of work that don't have direct analogues to what has been traditionally understood to be humanities scholarship. Digital humanities scholars, such as Bethany Nowviskie, have argued vigorously against the move to "evaluate the products of digital scholarship as if they can be mapped neatly to unary objects and established categories, such as journal articles or monographs,"[22] but it is clear that many traditional humanities scholars continue to look for print analogues to digital objects. Equally problematic is the suggestion that digital projects are best valued by the publication of an essay or book discussing the project, another way to bypass a disciplinary culture shift in assessment. Resistance to valuing the tool, database, or code as scholarship in and of itself puts an extra burden on scholars working with digital production.

In 1989, R. G. Potter called for a revision of literary studies; "What we need is a principled use of technology and criticism to form a new kind of literary study absolutely comfortable with scientific methods yet completely suffused with the values of the humanities."[23] We need to work together, in the shared spaces, to develop working models that best articulate our hopes. If we do indeed believe in digital humanities as transformative then we must continue to excavate and to rebuild the structures that underpin our work and our community. Our scholarly work at the intersections of technology and humanities is important, but it is our work that challenges power structures that is crucial. DH might shift exclusionary practices that have long run roughshod over the best impulses of academia, but to shift practices we cannot become what we battle.

Notes

Introduction

1. Matthew Kirschenbaum, "What Is Digital Humanities and What's It Doing in English Departments?," *ADE Bulletin* 150 (2010): 55–61, 55.

2. For an extended history see Susan Hockey, "The History of Humanities Computing," in *A Companion to Digital Humanities*, ed. Susan Schreibman, Ray Siemens, and John Unsworth. (Malden, Oxford: Blackwell, 2004), 3–19.

3. Patrik Svensson, "Humanities Computing as Digital Humanities," *DHQ: Digital Humanities Quarterly* 3.3 (2009): n.p. http://www.digitalhumanities.org/dhq/vol/3/3/000065/000065.html.

4. Susan Hockey, "The History of Humanities Computing," 13.

5. Pockets of digital work in Europe continue to utilize the term humanities computing, but the term is all but extinct in the US academy.

6. Kirschenbaum, "What Is Digital Humanities and What's It Doing in English Departments?," 56–57.

7. "Day of DH: Defining the Digital Humanities," in *Debates in the Digital Humanities*, ed. Matthew K. Gold. (Minneapolis: U Minnesota P, 2011), 67–71, 68.

8. Susan Schreibman, Ray Siemens, and John Unsworth, eds., *A Companion to Digital Humanities* (Malden, Oxford: Blackwell, 2004). Ray Siemens and Susan Schreibman, eds. *A Companion to Digital Literary Studies* (Malden, Oxford: Blackwell, 2007). Willard McCarty, *Humanities Computing* (New York: Palgrave Macmillan, 2005). Jerome McGann, *Radiant Textuality: Literature After the World Wide Web* (New York: Palgrave, 2001).

9. David M. Berry, ed., *Understanding Digital Humanities* (Basingstoke: Palgrave Macmillan, 2012). Steven E. Jones, *The Emergence of the Digital Humanities* (New

York & London: Routledge, 2014). Kenneth M. Price and Ray Siemens, eds., *Literary Studies in the Digital Age: An Evolving Anthology* (New York: MLA Commons, 2013). http://dlsanthology.commons.mla.org. Anne Burdick et al., eds., *Digital Humanities* (Boston: MIT Press, 2012). Melissa Terras, Julianne Nyhan, and Edward Vanhoutte, eds., *Defining Digital Humanities: A Reader* (Surrey: Ashgate, 2013).

10. Susan Hockey, *Electronic Texts in the Humanities* (New York: Oxford UP, 2000). Daniel J. Cohen and Tom Scheinfeldt, *Hacking the Academy: New Approaches to Scholarship and Teaching from Digital Humanities* (Ann Arbor: U Michigan P, 2013). Matthew Jockers, *Macroanalysis: Digital Methods and Literary History* (Urbana, Chicago, and Springfield: U Illinois P, 2013).

11. Alan Liu, "Where Is Cultural Criticism in the Digital Humanities?," *Alan Liu*, January 7, 2011, http://liu.english.ucsb.edu/where-is-cultural-criticism-in-the-digital-humanities. John Unsworth, "What Is Humanities Computing and What Is Not?," May 1, 2009. http://computerphilologie.uni-muenchen.de/jg02/unsworth.html. Matthew Kirschenbaum, "What Is Digital Humanities and What's It Doing in English Departments?," 55–61. Bethany Nowviskie, "Eternal September of the Digital Humanities," *Bethany Nowviskie*, October 15, 2010. http://nowviskie.org/2010/eternal-september-of-the-digital-humanities.

Chapter 1

1. Modern Language Association, "Guidelines for Editors of Scholarly Editions," June 29, 2011. http://www.mla.org/cse_guidelines. I include projects such as the following in this subgroup: *Typee: Fluid Text Edition, The Electronic New Variorum Shakespeare, The Canterbury Tales Project, The Electronic Beowulf, The Thomas MacGreevy Archive, Piers Plowman*, and *The Digital Watermark & Ornament Catalogue*.

2. I am well aware of the blurriness of the term "textual studies," recognizing that who is in and who is out depends upon the scholar's understanding of "text." Some traditional bibliographic scholars believe that enumerative bibliography, and in some cases, descriptive and annotated bibliography, fall outside of the purview of textual studies. This chapter will provide a broad overview of the tensions within textual studies during the period of the digital edition.

3. "The Society for Textual Scholarship and Textual Cultures," *About the Society for Textual Scholarship and Textual Cultures*, June 2012. http://textualsociety.org/about.

4. Judith Kennedy, "'A Terrible Beauty is Born': Textual Scholarship in the 1990s," *Victorian Literature and Culture*, 21 (1993): 379–88 offers a clear and useful summary of the conflict within textual studies.

5. In this chapter I focus on those projects that emerge from the textual studies

milieu. Digital or etexts, such as those developed out of libraries and etext centers, will be discussed elsewhere in the volume. I exclude discussion of the various for-profit digitization projects, such as Chadwyck-Healey's *The English Poetry Full-Text Database* and Gale's *Eighteenth Century Collection Online (ECCO)*. The for-profit industry has different structures and concerns and it would be most beneficial to address these issues elsewhere.

6. See W. Speed Hill, "Editorial Theory and Literary Criticism: Lamb and Wolf?," *Review* 19 (1997): 37–61 for additional history.

7. D.C. Greetham, *Textual Scholarship: An Introduction* (New York and London: Garland, 1994), 334–35.

8. G. Thomas Tanselle, *A Rationale of Textual Criticism* (Philadelphia: U Pennsylvania P, 1989), 69.

9. Proctor Williams and Craig S. Abbott, *An Introduction to Bibliographical and Textual Studies* (New York: The Modern Language Association of America, 1985), 6.

10. Tanselle, *A Rationale of Textual Criticism*, 21. *Studies in Bibliography* became the leading scholarly journal through which the Greg-Bowers approach to editorial and bibliographical theory was defended.

11. George Bornstein, "Introduction," in *Palimpsest: Editorial Theory in the Humanities*, ed. George Bornstein and Ralph G. Williams (Ann Arbor: U Michigan P, 1993), 1–6, 3.

12. Jacques Derrida, *Archive Fever: A Freudian Impression* (Chicago: U Chicago P, 1996), 69.

13. G. Thomas Tanselle, "Textual Criticism and Deconstruction," *Studies in Bibliography* 43 (1989): 1–33, 4.

14. Tanselle, "Textual Criticism and Deconstruction," 1.

15. D.C. Greetham, *Textual Scholarship: An Introduction* (New York and London: Garland, 1994), 1.

16. Michael Groden, "Contemporary Textual and Literary Theory," in *Representing Modernist Texts: Editing as Interpretation*, ed. George Bornstein (Ann Arbor: U Michigan P, 1991), 259–86, 259.

17. Edmund Wilson, "The Fruits of MLA," in *The Devils and Canon Barham: Ten Essays on Poets, Novelists and Monsters* (New York: Farrar, Straus and Giroux, 1973), 154–202, 170.

18. Ian Small, "Identifying Text and Postmodernist Editorial Projects," *The Yearbook of English Studies* 29 (1999): 43–56, 48.

19. Leroy R. Searle, "Emerging Questions: Text and Theory in Contemporary Criticism," *Voice, Text, Hypertext: Emerging Practices in Textual Studies*, ed. Raimonda Modiano, Leroy Searle, and Peter Shillingsburg (Seattle: U Washington P, 2004), 3–21, 3.

20. See Hans Walter Gabler, "Unsought Encounters," *Devils and Angels: Textual Editing and Literary Theory*, ed. Philip G. Cohen (Charlottesville: UP Virginia, 1991), 152–66, 26; Jerome J. McGann, "The Monks and the Giants: Textual and Bibliographical Studies and the Interpretation of Literary Works," in *Textual Criticism and Literary Interpretation* (Chicago: U Chicago P, 1985), 27; and G. Thomas Tanselle, *A Rationale of Textual Criticism* (Philadelphia: U Pennsylvania P, 1989).

21. Robert D. Hume, "The Aims and Uses of 'Textual Studies,'" *PBSA* 99.2 (2005): 197–230, 197.

22. Hume, "The Aims and Uses of 'Textual Studies,'" 199.

23. Hans Walter Gabler, "Textual Studies and Criticism," *The Library Chronicle of the University of Texas at Austin* 20.1–2 (1990): 151–65, 152.

24. Jerome McGann, *A Critique of Modern Textual Criticism* (Chicago: U Chicago P, 1983), 8.

25. D.C. Greetham, *Textual Scholarship: An Introduction*, 337.

26. Peter L. Shillingsburg, "Principles for Electronic Archives, Scholarly Editions, and Tutorials," in *The Literary Text in the Digital Age*, ed. Richard J. Finneran (Ann Arbor: U Michigan P, 1996), 23–35, 23.

27. One can only wish for a return to the prices that Shillingsburg quotes. Current prices for scholarly editions can range from around $100 to $800.

28. The scholarly publishing industry has only become less stable since the 2002 MLA report. Scholarly presses are closing, such as Rice and Missouri, and those that remain continue to struggle to find a sustainable economic model. Library funding is contracting yet scholars required to publish monographs to meet tenure and promotion criteria are growing.

29. MLA Ad Hoc Committee on the Future of Scholarly Publishing, "The Future of Scholarly Publishing," *Profession* (2002): 172–86, 176.

30. Richard J. Finneran, ed. *The Literary Text in the Digital Age* (Ann Arbor: U Michigan P, 1996), ix.

31. D. C. Greetham, "Editorial and Critical Theory: From Modernism to Postmodernism," in *Palimpsest: Editorial Theory in the Humanities*, ed. George Bornstein and Ralph G. Williams (Ann Arbor: U Michigan P, 1993), 9–28, 17.

32. G. Thomas Tanselle, "Print History and Other History," *Studies in Bibliography* 48 (1995): 268–89, 288.

33. Michigan's "The Editorial Theory and Literary Criticism" series' editorial board members, George Bornstein, Jerome McGann, Peter Shillingsburg, Hans Gabler, A. Walton Litz, and JoAnn Boydston, have nurtured discussions about both textual studies and the digital, with a good number of the series' publications dedicated to issuing involving the digital.

34. Also interesting is the decision, in 1995, to convert *Studies in Bibliography* to

a digital format. The journal was brought online by the University of Virginia Etext Center and is now part of Project Muse.

35. MLA Committee for Scholarly Editing, "Guidelines for Editors of Scholarly Editions."

36. Peter Shillingsburg, "How Literary Works Exist: Convenient Scholarly Editions," *DHQ: Digital Humanities Quarterly* 3.3 (2009): n.p.

37. I will discuss this fragmentation in chapter 4. Peter Shillingsburg, *From Gutenberg to Google: Electronic Representations of Literary Texts* (Cambridge: Cambridge UP, 2006), 23–24.

38. Peter L. Shillingsburg, *Scholarly Editing in the Computer Age: Theory and Practice*, 1st ed. (Athens and London: U Georgia P, 1986), 18.

39. David Greetham lambasts the decision to invite Tanselle to write the introduction for the *Electronic Textual Editing* volume. Greetham wonders, "Are the contributors aware that many of their arguments and practices are being undercut by the Forward?" (Greetham, "Review Electronic Textual Editing," 133). While there is no doubt that Tanselle spent a good portion of his career attacking the textual editors represented in the book, I would argue that much of the textual studies form that is replicated in digital humanities work during this period would be to Tanselle's liking. It is the experimental work in digital textual studies that he clearly rejects.

40. G. Thomas Tanselle, "TEI: Foreword," in *Electronic Textual Editing: Critical Editing in a Digital Horizon*, ed. Dino Buzzetti and Jerome McGann (New York: The Modern Language Association of America, 2006), 1–6, 3.

41. W. Speed Hill, "From 'an age of editing' to a 'paradigm shift': An Editorial Retrospect," *Text* 16 (2006): 33–47, 43.

42. David Gants, "The CUP Ben Jonson: Ruminations of the Electronic Edition," *Ben Jonson Journal* 5 (1998): 271–81, 275.

43. Peter Robinson, "Where We Are with Electronic Scholarly Editions, and Where We Want to Be," *Forum Computerphilologie*. http://computerphilologie.uni-muenchen.de/jg03/robinson.html.

44. Peter Shillingsburg, "How Literary Works Exist: Convenient Scholarly Editions," *DHQ: Digital Humanities Quarterly* 3.3 (2009): n.p.

45. W. Speed Hill, "Editorial Theory and Literary Criticism: Lamb and Wolf?," 43.

46. Kevin Kiernan, "The Electronic Beowulf Project." *The Calgary Electric Scriptorium*. http://people.ucalgary.ca/~scriptor/kiernan/calgary.html.

47. Kevin Kiernan, "The Electronic Beowulf Project."

48. Kevin Kiernan, "Electronic Beowulf." http://www.uky.edu/~kiernan/eBeowulf/ guide.htm.

49. Joseph Viscomi, "Digital Facsimiles: Reading the William Blake Archive," *Computers and the Humanities* 36 (2002): 27–48, 30.

50. "The Archive at a Glance," *The William Blake Archive*. http://www.blakearchive.org/blake/public/about/glance/index.html.

51. "Editorial Principles: Methodology and Standards in the Blake Archive," *The William Blake Archive*. http://www.blakearchive.org/blake/public/about/principles/index.html.

52. Philip Cohen, "Is There a Text in This Discipline? Textual Scholarship and American Literary Studies," *American Literary History* 8.4 (1996): 728–44, 730–31.

53. Hoyt N. Duggan and Richard K. Emmerson, "Medieval Academy Electronic Publications: SEENET and Beyond," *Medieval Academy News* (2004): n.p.

54. Duggan and Emmerson, "Medieval Academy Electronic Publications."

55. More recent digital edition projects have resisted such rigid approaches to the text. Both the *Electronic Shakespeare Variorum* and John Bryant's Melville's *Typee* represent projects that allow textual manipulation by the user. Bryant is interested in revealing the fluidity of text and, as such, uses the digital environment as a way to make not only the textual condition apparent but to "make the editorial process more understandable and accessible to everyday users" (Interview). He notes in his 2008 NEH grant application for the project, "If the genre of the 'eclectic edition' has faded, today's editorial goal of analyzing variants to clarify the stages of an author's fluid text, revision practices, and shifting (not fixed) intentions will surely be more fully realized through online critical archives such as the proposed MEL." John Bryant, "The Melville Electronic Library." http://mel.hofstra.edu/pdf/neh_grant_2009–11.pdf. A central goal of the project, to reveal the variants, is crucial to the construction of the interface that reveals the apparatus. Alan Galey's similar experiment with apparatus construction in the *Electronic Variorum Shakespeare*, where the apparatus is coded to be manipulated by the reader, emphasizes a break from early digital edition fixity.

56. Peter Robinson, "Question Re Digital Editions" (2009): n.p.

57. Susan Hockey, "Creating and Using Electronic Editions," *The Literary Text in the Digital Age*, ed. Richard J. Finneran (Ann Arbor: U Michigan P, 1996), 1–21, 11.

58. The members were: Lou Burnard, Oxford University; David T. Barnard, Queen's University; David Chesnutt, University of South Carolina; Nancy Ide, Vassar College; and C.M. Sperberg-McQueen, University of Illinois at Chicago.

59. The Association for Computers and the Humanities Working Committee on Text Encoding Practices, "Proposal: For an NEH Grant of Emergency Funds" (1987): 1–27.

60. Lou Burnard and C.M. Sperberg-McQueen, "Living with the Guidelines: An Introduction to TEI Tagging." http://xml.coverpages.org/teiu5-uva.html.

61. See, for example, Marjorie Burghart and Malte Rehbeing, "The Present and Future of the TEI Community for Manuscript Encoding," *Journal of the Text Encoding Initiative* 2 (2012): n.p. http://jtei.revues.org/372.

62. G. Thomas Tanselle, "Historicism and Critical Editing," *Studies in Bibliography* 39 (1986): 1–46, 4.

63. The Association for Computers and the Humanities Working Committee on Text Encoding Practices, 15.

64. ADE was the site of the ugly scene of disciplinary tension when, in 1978, G. Thomas Tanselle delivered his talk, "The Editing of Historical Documents," in which he castigated historical editors.

65. Jerome McGann, "Electronic Archives and Critical Editing," *Literature Compass* 7.2 (2010): 37–42, 41.

66. TEI Consortium, "An Agreement to Establish a Consortium for the Maintenance of the Text Encoding Initiative." http://www.tei-c.org/About/consortium.html.

67. Steven E. Jones, Peter Shillingsburg, and George K. Thiruvathukal, "E-Carrel: An Environment for Collaborative Textual Scholarship," *Journal of the Chicago Colloquium on Digital Humanities and Computer Science* 1.2 (2010): 1–12, 2.

68. Peter Shillingsburg, "How Literary Works Exist: Convenient Scholarly Editions," *DHQ: Digital Humanities Quarterly* 3.3 (2009): n.p.

69. Kenneth Price, "Electronic Scholarly Editions," in *A Companion to Digital Literary Studies*, ed. Ray Siemens and Susan Schreibman (Malden, Oxford: Blackwell, 2007), 434–50, 434.

70. John Bryant's current digital editing work has helped to broaden such work. His *Herman Melville's Typee: A Fluid-Text Edition* (U Virginia P, 2006) was the second digital edition, after Blake, to be given approval by the MLA Committee for Scholarly Editing.

71. Ian Small, "Identifying Text and Postmodernist Editorial Projects," *The Yearbook of English Studies* 29 (1999): 43–56, 43.

72. Jerome J. McGann, "The Monks and the Giants: Textual and Bibliographical Studies and the Interpretation of Literary Works," 190.

73. Margaret J.M. Ezell, "Editing Early Modern Women's Manuscripts: Theory, Electronic Editions, and the Accidental Copy-Text," *Literature Compass* 7.2 (2010): 102–9, 107.

74. Martha Nell Smith. "The Human Touch: Software of the Highest Order: Revisiting Editing as Interpretation," *Textual Cultures* 2.1 (2007): 1–15, 2.

75. Smith, "The Human Touch," 4.

76. Julia Flanders, "The Body Encoded: Questions of Gender and the Electronic Text," in *Electronic Text: Investigations in Method and Theory*, ed. Kathryn Sutherland (London: Oxford UP, 1997), 127–43, 129.

77. Flanders, "The Body Encoded," 129.

78. Fredson Bowers, *Textual and Literary Criticism* (Cambridge: Cambridge UP, 1959). Thank you to Maura Ives for suggesting this line of thinking.

79. G. Thomas Tanselle, "The Life and Work of Fredson Bowers," *Studies in Bibliography* 46 (1993): 1–155, 21.

Chapter 2

1. Stephen Greenblatt, *Marvelous Possessions: The Wonder of the New World* (Chicago: U Chicago P, 1991), 3.

2. For example, Wesley Raabe and Les Harrison's *A Selection from* Uncle Tom's Cabin: *A Digital Critical Edition; "Topsy," Scholarly Editing* 33 (2012): http://www.scholarlyediting.org/2012/editions/utctopsy/intro.utctopsy.html is an edition, rather than an archive, as the project is invested in tracking textual variants and transmission.

3. I am not suggesting that all of these scholars would consider themselves new historicists but that certain aspects of their scholarship draw upon new historicist methodologies.

4. Jeffrey N. Cox and Larry J. Reynolds, "The Historicist Enterprise," in *New Historical Literary Study: Essays on Reproducing Texts, Representing History*, ed. Jeffrey N. Cox and Larry J. Reynolds (Princeton: Princeton UP, 1993), 3–38, 3.

5. H. Aram Veeser, ed., *The New Historicism Reader* (New York: Routledge, 1994), 2–3.

6. Louis Montrose, "Professing the Renaissance: The Poetics and Politics of Cultures," *The New Historicism*, ed. H. Aram Veeser (New York and London: Routledge, 1989), 15–36, 15.

7. Stephen Greenblatt, "Towards a Poetics of Culture," *The New Historicism*, ed. H. Aram Veeser (New York and London: Routledge, 1989), 1–14, 1.

8. Donald J. Waters, "Archives, Online Edition-Making, and the Future of Scholarly Communication in the Humanities," *The Changing Landscape of Scholarly Communication in the Digital Age*, Texas A&M University, February 11, 2009. http://futureofpublishing.tamu.edu/program/symposium-program.html.

9. Jerome McGann, *Radiant Textuality: Literature after the World Wide Web* (New York: Palgrave, 2001), 11–12.

10. McGann, *Radiant Textuality*, 12.

11. Jerome McGann discusses the beginnings of IATH in the introduction to *Radiant Textuality.*

12. McGann, *Radiant Textuality*, 10.

13. McGann. *Radiant Textuality*, 15.

14. Compare the history of the *WWA* and *RA* to that of George Landow's *The Dickens Web*, now a product distributed by Eastgate systems, the same publisher of early eliterature texts including Michael Joyce's *afternoon, a story.* Kenneth M. Price, "The Walt Whitman Archive at Ten: Some Backward Glances and Vistas Ahead," *Mickle Street Review* (2005): n.p. http://www.whitmanarchive.org/about/articles/anc.00008.html.

15. *The Rossetti Archive*, as it has come to be known, was given the full name: *The Complete Writings and Pictures of Dante Gabriel Rossetti.* The digital, by itself, has not solved the questions that McGann calls forth in his work. McGann continues to push for new digital representations of text, noting that the *RA* was an experiment to learn from rather than the end product of his imagining.

16. Jerome McGann, "The Rationale of Hypertext," Institute for Advanced Technology in the Humanities. http://www2.iath.virginia.edu/jjm2f/rationale.htm.

17. Marilyn Levinson et al., *Rethinking Historicism: Critical Readings in Romantic History* (Oxford: Basil Blackwell, 1989), 20.

18. Jacques Derrida, *Archive Fever: A Freudian Impression* (Chicago: U Chicago P, 1996), 11.

19. Matthew G. Kirschenbaum, "Special Cluster: Done," *DHQ: Digital Humanities Quarterly* 3.2 (2009): n.p.

20. Susan Brown et al., "Published Yet Never Done: The Tension Between Projection and Completion in Digital Humanities Research," *DHQ: Digital Humanities Quarterly* 3.2 (2009): n.p.

21. Catherine Gallagher and Stephen Greenblatt, *Practicing New Historicism* (Chicago: U Chicago P, 2000), 21.

22. See Gallagher and Greenblatt, *Practicing New Historicism.*

23. Levinson et al., *Rethinking Historicism*, 20.

24. Brook Thomas, "Figuring the Relation Between Literary and Cultural Histories," *The Yearbook of Research in English and American Literature* 17 (2001): 341–57, 341–42.

25. Veeser, *The New Historicism*, ix.

26. Jerome McGann, interview, April 16, 2010.

27. W. Speed Hill, "From 'an age of editing' to a 'paradigm shift': An Editorial Retrospect," *Text* 16 (2006): 33–47, 40.

28. Sonja Laden, "Recuperating the Archive: Anecdotal Evidence and Questions of 'Historical Realism,'" *Poetics Today* 25.1 (2004): 1–28, 7.

29. Jacques Derrida and Eric Prenowitz, "Archive Fever: A Freudian Impression," *Diacritics* 25.2 (1995): 9–63, 10.

30. Derrida and Prenowitz, 10.

31. Cox and Reynolds, "The Historicist Enterprise," 4.

32. John Unsworth, "Digital Surrogates for the Printed Book: Problems and Possibilities," The Seventh International Conference of the Society for Emblem Studies, July 25, 2005. http://www3.isrl.illinois.edu/~unsworth/emblems.05.html.

33. Stuart Hall, "Foucault: Power, Knowledge, and Discourse," *Discourse Theory and Practice: A Reader*, ed. Margaret Wetherell et al. (London: SAGE, 2001), 72–81, 75.

34. Michel Foucault, *Power/Knowledge: Selected Interviews and Other Writings, 1972–1977*, ed. Colin Gordon (New York: Vintage, 1980), 196.

35. Folsom argues that the *WWA* and other such archives are databases and, as such, new literary genres. Ed Folsom, "Database as Genre: The Epic Transformation of Archives," *PMLA* 122.5 (2007): 1571–79.

36. Jerome McGann, "Database, Interface, and Archival Fever," *PMLA* 122.5 (2007): 1588–92, 1588.

37. Margaret J.M. Ezell, "Paraplex: Or, the Functions of Angels in the Archives," Women Writers Project Conference, March 5–7, 2009, n.p. http://www.wwp.brown.edu/outreach/conference/wia2009/papers/ezell.html.

38. Dana Wheeles, "Testing NINES," *Literary and Linguistic Computing* 25.4 (2010): 393–403, 393.

39. NINES website, accessed June 25, 2010. http://www.nines.org.

40. NINES website, accessed March 15, 2014. http://www.nines.org.

41. Kenneth M. Price, "Edition, Project, Database, Archive, Thematic Research Collection: What's in a Name?," *DHQ: Digital Humanities Quarterly* 3.3 (2009): n.p., accessed April 7, 2010. http://digitalhumanities.org/dhq/vol/3/3/000053/000053.html.

42. Katherine L. Walter and Kenneth M. Price, "An Online Guide to Walt Whitman's Dispersed Manuscripts," *The Walt Whitman Archive*, n.p. http://www.whitmanarchive.org/about/articles/anc.00001.html.

43. Ed Folsom, "Projecting Whitman: The Evolution and Remediation of the Collected Writings of Walt Whitman—The Walt Whitman Archive," *The Walt Whitman Archive*, n.p., accessed March 3, 2010. http://www.whitmanarchive.org/about/articles/anc.00003.html.

44. Jane Tompkins, *Sensational Designs: The Cultural Work of American Fiction, 1790–1860* (New York: Oxford UP, 1985), xi.

45. Tompkins, *Sensational Designs*, 126.

46. Laden, "Recuperating the Archive," 13.

47. Laden, "Recuperating the Archive," 13.

48. Liu, *Local Transcendent*, 259.

49. Liu, *Local Transcendent*, 260.

50. Cox and Reynolds, "The Historicist Enterprise," 4.

51. Ezell, "Paraplex," n.p.

52. The TEI is a set of metadata standards that are specifically designed to encode literary and digital texts. Such standards allow the computer to interpret and manipulate textual materials, making the TEI important to those that are interested in treating a text as data for interpretation.

53. Martha Nell Smith, "Because the Plunge from the Front Overturned Us: The Dickinson Electronic Archives Project," *Studies in the Literary Imagination* 32.1 (1999): 133–51, 135–36.

54. Dave Parry, "Be Online or Be Irrelevant," *AcademHack*, January 11, 2010, accessed January 11, 2010. http://academhack.outsidethetext.com/home/2010/be-online-or-be-irrelevant.

55. Edward L. Ayers, "The Pasts and Futures of Digital History: Edward L. Ayers," Virginia Center for Digital History, 199, accessed July 15, 2009. http://www.vcdh.virginia.edu/PastsFutures.html.

56. Daniel Cohen, "The Pirate Problem," *Dan Cohen*, April 22, 2008, accessed July 17, 2009. http://www.dancohen.org/2008/04/22/the-pirate-problem.

57. Historians are not the only group that sees their discipline as specially positioned within digital humanities. Matthew Kirschenbaum has noted, "digital humanities has accumulated a robust professional apparatus that is probably more rooted in English than any other departmental home." Kirschenbaum, "What Is Digital Humanities and What's It Doing In English Departments?," 1.

58. Joe Moran, *Interdisciplinarity* (London: Routledge, 2002), 4.

59. Moran, *Interdisciplinarity*, 114.

60. Moran, *Interdisciplinarity*, 184.

61. Moran, *Interdisciplinarity*, 48.

62. Montrose, "Professing the Renaissance," 19.

63. Carolyn Steedman, *Dust: The Archive and Cultural History* (New Brunswick: Rutgers UP, 2002), 68.

Chapter 3

1. Sandra M. Gilbert and Susan Gubar, *The Madwoman in the Attic: The Woman Writer and the Nineteenth-Century Literary Imagination* (New Haven: Yale UP, 1979).

2. Sandra M. Gilbert and Susan Gubar, *The Norton Anthology of Literature by Women: The Tradition in English* (New York: Norton, 1985).

3. Margaret J.M. Ezell, *Writing Women's Literary History* (Baltimore: Johns Hopkins UP, 1993), 15.

4. "Battle for the Soul of the Internet," *Time Magazine*, July 25, 1994.

5. Peter Childers and Paul Delany, "Introduction: Two Versions of Cyberspace," *Works and Days* 23.4 (1994): 61–78.

6. J. D. Bolter, *Writing Space: The Computer, Hypertext, and the History of Writing* (Boston: Houghton Mifflin, 1991), 233.

7. Peter L. Shillingsburg, "Principles for Electronic Archives, Scholarly Editions, and Tutorials," *The Literary Text in the Digital Age*, ed. Richard J. Finneran (Ann Arbor: U Michigan P, 1996): 23–35, 25.

8. Fan sites and other nonscholarly produced materials were recovering texts but are not discussed in this chapter, primarily because the materials are not particularly reliable. The same is true of large-scale digitization projects including Project Gutenberg. For additional information regarding the problems with such materials, see Peter Shillingsburg, *From Gutenberg to Google: Electronic Representations of Literary Texts* (Cambridge: Cambridge UP, 2006).

9. *The 19th Century American Women Writers Web (19CWWW)* was a collective project developed by scholars including Tyler Steben, Janice Milner Lasseter, Janet S. Gray, Dwayne Best, Eric Gardner, Gran McEntee, Judy Boss, and others that included art, literature, and medicine. Various partnerships included the Carnegie Museum and Henry Ford Museum/Greenfield Village. The remains of the project, selected literature texts, are currently housed on the Society for the Study of American Women Writers page at http://www.lehigh.edu/~dek7/SSAWW/eTextLib.htm. No other archive has been preserved, leaving our knowledge of the site derived from archived posts on the listserv h-net. Developed in 1996 by Toni McNaron and Carol Miller, *Voices from the Gaps* remains an active site, located at http://voices.cla.umn.edu. *Early American Women Writers* was created by Sharon Harris and was removed from the web in 2011. *The Black Poetry Page* is listed in the *Heath Anthology Guide, Volume II* and included poetry from Arna Bontemps and Claude McKay. No archive currently exists, though we do know that the site was published at the University of Pennsylvania. *The Online Archive of Nineteenth-Century U.S. Women's Writings*, indexed by MLA, was edited by Glynnis Carr and exists at http://www.facstaff.bucknell.edu/gcarr/19cusww/index.html. *American Women Writers 1890 to 1939—Modernism and Mythology* was created by Kristin Mapel-Bloomberg to supplement her book *Tracing Arachne's Web: Myth and Feminist Fiction*. The site was removed in 2008, though the Internet archive retains copies of the site.

10. Since the materials are housed on a personal university website, controlled by a retired faculty member, the bibliography is in clear danger of being lost.

11. Judith Fetterley, "Judith Fetterley Personal Web Page." http://www.albany.edu/~jf/index.html.

12. Fetterley, "Judith Fetterley Personal Web Page."

13. Fetterley, "Judith Fetterley Personal Web Page."

14. Susan Fraiman, "In Search of Our Mother's Gardens—With Help from a New Digital Resource for Literary Scholars," *Modern Philology* 106.1 (2008): 142–48, 143.

15. Neil Fraistat, Steven E. Jones, and Carl Stahmer, "The Canon, The Web, and the Digitization of Romanticism," *Romanticism on the Net* 10 (1998): n.p.

16. Neil Fraistat, Steven E. Jones, and Carl Stahmer, "The Canon, The Web, and the Digitization of Romanticism."

17. Amy Spencer, *DIY: The Rise of Lo-Fi Culture* (London: Marion Boyars, 2008), 11.

18. *Riot GRRL manifesto*. http://onewarart.org/riot_grrrl_manifesto.htm.

19. Ryan Moore and Michael Roberts, "Do-It-Yourself Mobilization: Punk and Social Movements," *Mobilization: An International Quarterly* 14.3 (2009): 273–91, 288.

20. *Native Web* is still online, though the numbers of links to literature have decreased over time, suggesting that relevant projects have disappeared from the web. http://nativeweb.org.

21. Alan Liu launched *The Voice of the Shuttle* in 1994. http://vos.ucsb.edu. Randy Bass launched *The American Studies Crossroads Project* in 1993. http://crossroads. georgetown.edu.

22. *American Writers* is now *American Authors*. Still run by Donna M. Campbell, the site is located at http://public.wsu.edu/~campbelld.

23. Interview with Donna Campbell, September 2, 2011.

24. "Domestic Goddess" was begun in 1999 by Kim Wells.

25. Kim Wells, "Domestic Goddesses." http://www.womenwriters.net/domesticgoddess.

26. Neither site is still online. Archived sites are available through the Wayback Machine.

27. According to the 1994 Directory of Electronic Text Centers, the following centers were active in the United States: Columbia University, Dartmouth College, Emory University, Georgetown University, Harvard University, the University of Illinois, Urbana/Champaign, the University of Indiana, the University of Iowa, Johns Hopkins University, the University of Michigan, the New York Public Library, New York University, North Carolina State University, the University of Oregon, the University of Pennsylvania, a joint venture by Rutgers University and Princeton University, the University of Virginia, West Virginia University, and Yale University. Mary Mallery, Directory of Electronic Text Centers, August 9, 1994. http://www9.georgetown.edu/faculty/jod/etextcenters.

28. The *Walt Whitman Archive*, *Mark Twain in his Times*, and *Uncle Tom's Cabin*

& American Culture were initiated in IATH, but some of the digitization work for the projects was conducted by the Etext Center. See http://www.digitalcurationservices.org/digital-stewardship-services/etext-projects for a complete list of projects.

29. Laura Mandell and Michael Gamer, "On Romanticism, the Canon, and the Web—A Special Issue of Romanticism on the Net," *Romanticism on the Net* 10 (1998): n.p.

30. The biracial author Eaton (pen name Onoto Watanna) published *Miss Nume of Japan* in 1898, making her the first person of Asian descent to publish a novel in the United States and "the first Asian American to reach a national mainstream reading audience." Jean Lee Cole, "Newly Recovered Works by Onoto Watanna (Winnifred Eaton): A Prospectus and Checklist," *Legacy: A Journal of American Women Writers* 21.2 (2004): 229–34, 229. The *Winnifred Eaton Digital Archive* was originally published on the Etext Center at http://etext.lib.virginia.edu/eaton. By 2010 the archive had been absorbed into the UVA catalogue.

31. Interview with Jean Lee Cole, September 2011.

32. Kenneth M. Price, "Digital Scholarship, Economics, and the American Literary Canon," *Literature Compass* 6.2 (2009): 274–90.

33. The advent of Google Books would also have an impact on digitization projects. While Google Books has successfully digitized a great number of texts, scholars have discussed the problems with Google's digitization approaches, which include concerns about copyright, reliability, and coverage. See Geoffrey Nunberg and Peter Shillingsburg for additional discussion of this issue. Ultimately, Google Books is only reproducing texts that are already on library shelves. Texts that libraries do not purchase are not digitized, which leads to gaps in coverage, particularly gaps in coverage of unrepresented authors.

34. Using JSTOR Data for Research, I narrowed year of publication to 1950–2014. I searched for "canon" in the humanities subject group. For additional information see http://dfr.jstor.org.

35. The Wayback Machine is available at http://web.archive.org.

36. Email correspondence, March 25, 2014.

37. Nowviskie interview, February 9, 2009.

38. It is likely that the images would require copyright permissions that were not secured for the first archival version.

39. It is possible that the nonpublic metadata has preserved this information. However, it is not available to the user.

40. Jean Lee Cole, creator of the *WEDA*, wrote a blog post to try to remedy the loss of the archive. She reproduces a bibliography of Eaton's work with links to the UVA digital texts. While Cole creates a stopgap measure, we now have what is in

effect another edition of the *WEDA* rather than preservation of the original site. http://jeanleecole.wordpress.com/winnifred-eaton-digital-archive.

41. Angela Courtney and Michelle Dalmau, "*Victorian Women Writers Project* Resurrected," October 14, 2009. http://www.dlib.indiana.edu/education/brown-bags/fall2009/vwwp/vwwp_fall2009_brownbag.pdf.

42. "Encoding Overview," *Victorian Women Writers Project.* http://webapp1.dlib. indiana.edu/vwwp/projectinfo/encoding.do.

43. "The Brown University *Women Writers Project*." http://www.wwp.brown. edu.

44. This is not to suggest that the project has a fully secure future. Run primarily on soft money, the *WWP* has a more tenuous position than it would probably like.

45. Susanne Woods, "Recovering the Past, Discovering the Future: The Brown University Women Writers Project," *The South Central Review* 11.2 (1994): 17–23, 22.

46. Matthew G. Kirschenbaum, *Mechanisms: New Media and the Forensic Imagination* (Cambridge, MA: MIT Press, 2008), 264.

47. *Early American Women Writers.* http://www.eaww.uconn.edu/main_pages/homepage.html.

48. *Women of Color in Accounting.* https://www.facebook.com/womenofcolorinaccounting/timeline.

49. *Exquisite Family Records.* http://exquisites.org/exquisite-family/okiku-san. html.

50. Price, "Digital Scholarship, Economics, and the American Literary Canon," 275.

51. Email, March 25, 2014.

52. Amanda Gailey and Andrew Jewell, "Editors' Introduction to the First Issue of *Scholarly Editing: The Annual of the Association for Documentary Editing," Scholarly Editing* 33 (2012): 1–7.

53. Ezell, "Editing Early Modern Women's Manuscripts: Theory, Electronic Editions, and the Accidental Copy-Text," 107.

54. Martha Nell Smith, "The Human Touch: Software of the Highest Order: Revisiting Editing as Interpretation," *Textual Cultures* 2.1 (2007): 1–15, 4.

55. John Willinsky, "Toward the Design of an Open Monograph Press," *The Journal of Electronic Publishing* 12.1 (2009).

56. Kenneth M. Price, "Dollars and Sense in Collaborative Digital Scholarship: The Example of the Walt Whitman Hypertext Archive," *Documentary Editing* 23.2 (2001): 29–33, 43.

57. Price, "Digital Scholarship, Economics, and the American Literary Canon," 280.

58. Ezell, "Editing Early Modern Women's Manuscripts: Theory, Electronic Editions, and the Accidental Copy-Text."

59. Though materials are available digitally, quality is varied. For example, see Peter Shillingsburg, *From Gutenberg to Google: Electronic Representations of Literary Texts* (Cambridge: Cambridge UP, 2006).

60. Daniel J. Cohen, "The Future of Preserving the Past," *CRM: The Journal of Heritage Stewardship* (2005): 6–19.

61. Jerome McGann, "Culture and Technology: The Way We Live Now, What Is To Be Done?," *New Literary History* 36.1 (2005): 71–82, 72.

Chapter 4

1. Stephen Ramsay, "Algorithmic Criticism," in *A Companion to Digital Literary Studies*, ed. Susan Schreibman, Ray Siemens, and John Unsworth (Malden, Oxford: Blackwell, 2008), 477–91, 477–78, 484.

2. Matthew Jockers, *Macroanalysis: Digital Methods and Literary History* (Urbana, Chicago, and Springfield: U Illinois P, 2013), 15.

3. Much of the discussion regarding the future of digital literary studies is happening between scholars in a plethora of departments across national boundaries. While I continue to use digital literary studies within the United States as the boundary for my project, this chapter is broader than the previous chapters.

4. Jerome McGann, *Radiant Textuality: Literature after the World Wide Web* (New York: Palgrave, 2001), xii.

5. John M. Unsworth, "Tool-Time, or 'Haven't We Been Here Already?,'" "Transforming Disciplines: The Humanities and Computer Science," Saturday, January 18, 2003. Washington, DC. http://people.lis.illinois.edu/~unsworth/carnegie-ninch.03.html.

6. It is worth noting that the call for interpretive technologies has radiated from those who were at the University of Virginia in the early to mid-2000s.

7. Stephen Ramsay, "High Performance Computing for English Majors," *Stephen Ramsay*, 2006. http://lenz.unl.edu/papers/2008/04/14/high-performance-computing-for-english-majors.html.

8. "Summit on Digital Tools for the Humanities: Report on Summit Accomplishments" (Charlottesville, Virginia, 2006), 3.

9. John Bradley, "Text Tools." In *A Companion to Digital Humanities*, ed. Susan Schreibman, Ray Siemens, and John Unsworth (Malden, Oxford: Blackwell, 2004), 505–22, 506.

10. See the Bamboo Dirt wiki for a list of digital humanities tools. http://dirt.projectbamboo.org.

11. Johanna Drucker, "Humanistic Theory and Digital Scholarship." In *Debates in the Digital Humanities*, ed. Matthew K. Gold (St. Paul: U Minnesota P, 2012) 85–95, 85.

12. Johanna Drucker, "Humanistic Theory and Digital Scholarship," 94.

13. "Summit on Digital Tools for the Humanities: Report on Summit Accomplishments" (Charlottesville, Virginia, 2006), 4.

14. Susan Schreibman, "Re-Envisioning Versioning: A Scholar's Toolkit," in *Digital Philology and Mediaeval Text* (Pisas: Pacini editore, 2007), 93–102, 93.

15. Susan Schreibman, "Re-Envisioning Versioning: A Scholar's Toolkit," 97.

16. Susan Schreibman, "Re-Envisioning Versioning: A Scholar's Toolkit," 98.

17. A recent addition to JUXTA allows the user to export files to The Versioning Machine. Current development is underway to support a nuts-to-bolts digital edition builder.

18. Jerome McGann, "To the Nines," Slide 15 of 21. http://www.arl.org/arl-docs/events/fallforum/forum05/mcgann_files/mcgann.ppt.

19. Stephen Ramsay, "On Building," *Stephen Ramsay*. http://lenz.unl.edu/papers/2011/01/11/on-building.html.

20. Alan Galey and Stan Ruecker, "How a Prototype Argues," *Literary and Linguistic Computing* 25.4 (2010): 405–24, 407.

21. Stephen Ramsay and Geoffrey Rockwell, "Developing Things: Notes Toward an Epistemology of Building in the Digital Humanities," in *Debates in the Digital Humanities*, ed. Matthew K. Gold (U Minnesota P, 2011), 75–84, 83.

22. Stefan Sinclair, "Computer-Assisted Reading: Reconceiving Text Analysis," *Literary and Linguistic Computing* 18.2 (2003): 175–84, 178.

23. Stephen Ramsay, "In Praise of Pattern," Hamilton, ON, 2004. http://web.archive.org/web/20060302215711/http://cantor.english.uga.edu/docs/pattern.

24. Amanda Gailey and Andrew Jewell. "Putting the 'Humanities' Back in 'Digital Humanities': Scholarly Editing and the Promotion of Digital Textual Scholarship," 9–10.

25. Stephen Ramsay, "In Praise of Pattern."

26. Christine L. Borman, "The Digital Future is Now: A Call to Action for the Humanities," *DHQ: Digital Humanities Quarterly* 3.4 (2009): n.p.

27. Lisa Gitelman and Virginia Jackson, "Introduction," in *"Raw Data" Is an Oxymoron*, ed. Lisa Gitelman (Cambridge: MIT Press, 2013), 1–14, 3.

28. Geoffrey Rockwell, Conversation, Dublin, Ireland, 2012.

29. DIRT: Digital Research Tools Wiki. https://digitalresearchtools.pbworks.com/w/page/17801672/FrontPage.

30. "Mellon grant to fund project to develop data-mining software for libraries," *PsychCentral*, 2004, n.p.

31. Stan Ruecker et al., "Visualizing Repetition in Text," *Digital Studies* 1.2 (2009): n.p.

32. Martin Mueller, "TEI-Analytics and the MONK Project," TEI Members Meeting, 2008. http://www.cch.kcl.ac.uk/cocoon/tei2008/programme/abstracts/abstract-169.html.

33. Franco Moretti, *Graphs, Maps, Trees: Abstract Models for Literary History* (London and New York: Verso, 2005), 3–4.

34. Franco Moretti, *Graphs, Maps, Trees: Abstract Models for Literary History*, 1.

35. Katie Trumpener, "Critical Response I. Paratext and Genre System: A Response to Franco Moretti" *Critical Inquiry* 36.1 (2009): 159–71, 170.

36. Jane Gallop, "The Historicization of Literary Studies and the Fate of Close Reading," *Profession* (2007): 181–86.

37. Franco Moretti, "Critical Response: II. 'Relatively Blunt,'" *Critical Inquiry* 36.1 (2009), 172–74, 174.

38. Timothy Burke, "Franco Moretti: A Quantitative Turn for Cultural History?," *History News Network* (Blog), January 20, 2004. http://hnn.us/blogs/entries/3115.html.

39. John Unsworth and Martin Mueller, "The MONK Project Final Report," September 2, 2009, 5.

40. Tanya E. Clement, "'A thing not beginning and not ending': using digital tools to distant-read Gertrude Stein's *The Making of Americans*," *Literary and Linguistic Computing* 23.3 (2008): 361–81, 362.

41. Tanya Clement, "Text Analysis, Data Mining, and Visualizations in Literary Scholarship," *Literary Studies in the Digital Age: An Evolving Anthology*, ed. Kenneth M. Price and Ray Siemens (New York: MLA, 2013). http://dlsanthology.commons.mla.org/text-analysis-data-mining-and-visualizations-in-literary-scholarship.

42. Kevin D. Franklin and Karen Rodriguez'G, "The Next Big Thing in Humanities, Arts and Social Science Computing: 18thConnect," *HPCWire*, 2008. http://www.hpcwire.com/industry/academia/The_Next_Big_Thing_in_Humanities_Arts_and_Social_Science_Computing_18thConnect_35010199.html.

43. See chapter 3 for an extended discussion of the limited canon of digitized texts.

44. Kevin D. Franklin and Karen Rodriguez'G, "The Next Big Thing in Humanities, Arts and Social Science Computing: 18thConnect."

45. Optical Character Recognition or OCR is the translation of images to machine readable files.

46. Interview, Laura Mandell, by Allison Stevens. http://www.units.muohio.edu/english/People/Features/09Features/MandellLaura2–24–09.html.

47. Diana Kichuk, "Metamorphosis: Remediation in Early English Books Online (EEBO)," *Literary and Linguistic Computing* 22.3 (2007): 291–303.

48. Gale, "Catalog Reviews," 2010. http://www.gale.cengage.com/servlet/ReviewsServlet?region=9&imprint=745&type=4&id=GALEN7&titlecode=GALEN7.

49. Martin Mueller, "Scholarly Crowdsourcing of Early Modern Texts," *Mellon*, 2010.

50. John M. Unsworth and Martin Mueller, *The MONK Project Final Report*, 2009. http://www.monkproject.org/MONKprojectfinalreport.pdf.

51. Also note that MONK has limited their Wright fiction to three hundred texts.

52. In 2014, Indiana University released an updated version of *The Wright American Fiction*. http://webapp1.dlib.indiana.edu/TEIgeneral/welcome.do?brand=wright. The revision is an expansion on the original dataset, improving greatly the diversity of texts.

53. "Background," MONK. http://www.monkproject.org/background.html.

54. Matthew Wilkens, "The Geographic Imagination of Civil War-Era American Fiction," *American Literary History*, 25.4 (2013): 803–40.

55. Wright American Fiction, 1851–1875. http://www.letrs.indiana.edu/web/w/wright2/about.html.

56. James Harner, *MLA Literary Research Guide*, 5th ed. (New York: MLA, 2010).

57. Matthew Wilkens, "Canons, Close Readings, and the Evolution of Method," in *Debates in Digital Humanities*, ed. Matthew K. Gold (St Paul: U Minnesota P, 2012), 249–58, 252.

58. James Olney, "'I Was Born:' Slave Narratives, Their Status as Autobiography and as Literature," *Callaloo* 20 (1984): 46–73.

59. Olney, 48.

60. Ted Underwood, "Big but not distant," The Stone and the Shell, March 3, 2012. http://tedunderwood.com/2012/03/03/big-but-not-distant.

61. Roger Whitson, "DH, Archival Silence, and Linked Open Data," *Roger Whitson*. http://www.rogerwhitson.net/?p=1509.

62. Matthew G. Kirschenbaum, "Poetry, Patterns, and Provocation: The nora Project," *The Valve: A Literary Organ* (2006): n.p.

63. Lauren F. Klein, "The Image of Absence: Archival Silence, Data Visualization, and James Hemings," *American Literature* 85.4 (2013): 661–88.

64. Lauren F. Klein, "The Image of Absence: Archival Silence, Data Visualization, and James Hemings," 662.

65. Lauren F. Klein, "The Image of Absence: Archival Silence, Data Visualization, and James Hemings," 663, 665.

66. Klein adds an additional seven located letters to the fifty-one letters that reference Hemings or a member of his family found in the *Papers of Thomas Jefferson*.

67. Lauren F. Klein, "The Image of Absence: Archival Silence, Data Visualization, and James Hemings," 674.

68. Amanda French, "In Praise of Humanities Data," 2011. http://www.scribd.com/doc/50066437/In-Praise-of-Humanities-Data.

69. Stephen Ramsay, "In Praise of Pattern," *TEXT Technology* 2 (2005), 177–90, 189.

Chapter 5

1. Adam Kirsch, "Technology is Taking Over English Departments: The False Promise of the Digital Humanities," *The New Republic*, May 2, 2014. http://www.newrepublic.com/article/117428/limits-digital-humanities-adam-kirsc.

2. Matthew Kirschenbaum, "What Is 'Digital Humanities,' and Why Are They Saying Such Terrible Things about it?," *differences* 25.1 (2014): 46–63, 47.

3. Tom Scheinfeldt, "The Dividends of Difference: Recognizing Digital Humanities' Diverse Family Tree/s," *Found History*, April 7, 2014. http://www.foundhistory.org/2014/04/07/the-dividends-of-difference-recognizing-digital-humanities-diverse-family-trees.

4. Natalia Cecire, "When DH Was in Vogue: or, THATCamp Theory," *Works Cited*, October 19, 2011. http://nataliacecire.blogspot.com/2011/10/when-dh-was-in-vogue-or-thatcamp-theory.html.

5. Richard Grusin, "The Dark Side of Digital Humanities: Dispatches from Two Recent MLA Conventions," *differences* 15.2 (2014): 79–92, 86.

6. David Golumbia, "Death of a Discipline," *differences* 15.2 (2014): 156–76, 171.

7. Richard Grusin, "The Dark Side of Digital Humanities—Part 2," *Century for 21st Century Studies*, January 9, 2013. http://www.c21uwm.com/2013/01/09/dark-side-of-the-digital-humanities-part-2.

8. Lee Patterson, *Negotiating the Past: The Historical Understanding of Medieval Literature* (Madison: U Wisconsin P, 1987), 70.

9. Donald Pease, "Towards a Sociology of Literary Knowledge," in *Consequences of Theory*, ed. Jonathan Arac and Barbara Johnson (Baltimore: Johns Hopkins UP, 1991), 108–54, 119.

10. Walter Benn Michaels, "The Victims of New Historicism," *Modern Language Quarterly* 54:1 (1993): 111–20, 115.

11. William Pannapacker, "Digital Humanities Triumphant?," *Chronicle of Higher Education*, January 8, 2011. http://chronicle.com/blogs/brainstorm/pannapacker-at-mla-digital-humanities-triumphant/30915.

12. Lisa Spiro, "'This Is Why We Fight': Defining the Values of the Digital Humanities," in *Debates in the Digital Humanities*, ed. Matthew L. Gold (Minneapolis: U Minnesota P, 2012), 16–35, 16.

13. Stefan Sinclair, "Digital Humanities and Stardom," *Stefan Sinclair*, January 1, 2011. http://stefansinclair.name/dh-stardom.

14. Matthew Kirschenbaum, "The (DH) Stars Come Out in LA," *Matthew G. Kirschenbaum*, January 13, 2011. http://mkirschenbaum.wordpress.com/2011/01/13/the-dh-stars-come-out-in-la-2.

15. Roger Whitson, "Does DH Really Need to Be Transformed? My Reflections on #mla12," January 8, 2012. http://www.rogerwhitson.net/?p=1358.

16. Alan Liu, "Where Is Cultural Criticism in the Digital Humanities," *Alan Liu*.

17. Willard McCarty, Yale, the past and the future, Humanist listserv, February 2010.

18. Amanda Gailey, Yale, the past and the future, Humanist listserv, February 22, 2010.

19. Matthew Kirschenbaum, "What Is Digital Humanities and What's It Doing in English Departments?," *ADE Bulletin* 150 (2010): 1–7, 6.

20. Here I am well aware of the arguments that footnotes and acknowledgements represent working together in traditional humanities. However, I am arguing that DH represents a ground swell shift in working practices.

21. MLA, "Statement on Publication in Electronic Journals." http://www.mla.org/resources/documents/rep_it/statement_on_publica.

22. Bethany Nowviskie, "Where Credit Is Due: Preconditions for the Evaluation of Collaborative Digital Scholarship," *Profession* (2011): 169–81, 169.

23. R.G. Potter, "Introduction," in *Literary Computing and Literary Criticism: Theoretical and Practical Essays on Theme and Rhetoric*, ed. R.G. Potter (Philadelphia: U Pennsylvania P, 1989), xxix.

Index

activist presses, emergence of, 63–64
ADHO. *See* Alliance of Digital Humanities Organizations
Advanced Resource Consortium (ARC), 88
African American writers: *The Black Poetry Page*, 65, 140n9; inadequate coverage in digital datasets, 111; self-publication and increased visibility of, 70
African diaspora texts, preservation of, 88
Aggripa (A Book of the Dead), 82
algorithmic interpretation (technological interpretation), 9–10, 91; calls for, 91–92, 144n6; concepts central to, 93; and humanistic analysis, 105–6; possibilities of, 114–16, 125; visualization and, 100–106, 114
Alliance of Digital Humanities Organizations (ADHO), 3
The Ambrose Bierce Project, 39
American Documentary Editing group, 31
American Literature Association (ALA), 1996 San Diego meeting of, 38–39
The American Studies Crossroads Project, 71, 141n21
American Women Writers 1890 to 1939—Modernism and Mythology, 65, 73, 140n9

American Writers website, 71, 72f; technology standards and problems of, 84
anecdote, in new historicist scholarship, 54–55, 58
annotations, in scholarly editions, 19
ARC. *See* Advanced Resource Consortium
archives. *See* digital archives; viral archiving
Ashbaugh, Dennis, 82
Association for Computers and the Humanities, 2, 3; and TEI, 29
Association for Literary and Linguistic Computing, 2, 3
Ayers, Edward, 57, 124

Barnard, David, 30
Bass, Randy, 71, 141n21
Bauer, Jean, 123
Begos, Kevin, Jr., 82
Benstock, Shari, 73
Beowulf, digital edition of, 21, 24, 25f, 28
Berry, David M., 6
Best, Dwayne, 140n9
biases, tool, 106–107
bibliographic scholarship: vs. literary criticism, 17. *See also* textual studies
The Black Poetry Page, 65, 140n9
Blackwell Companion to Digital Humanities, 3, 5

Gabler, Hans, 17, 132n33
Gailey, Amanda: on future of digital
humanities, 124–125; and *Race and
Children's Literature of the Gilded Age*,
39; on technology standards, 84
Gale Group, 107, 131n5
Galey, Alan, 98, 134n55
Gallagher, Catherine, 38
Gallop, Jane, 102
Gamer, Michael, 74
Gants, David, 22–23, 74
Gardner, Eric, 140n9
Geertz, Clifford, 45
gender: early treatment in editing, 35–
36. *See also* women
Gibson, William, 82
Gilbert, Sandra M., 63
Gitelman, Lisa, 100
Gold, Matthew K., 6
Golumbia, David, 120–21
Google Books, digitization projects of,
107, 142n3; errors in, 108–9
Gray, Janet S., 140n9
Greenblatt, Stephen, 38; on new
historicism, 40, 41; "A Silk Road
Course," 39
Greetham, David (D. C.), 13, 15; on
digital environment and textual stud-
ies, 20; on *Electronic Textual Editing*,
133n39; on social text criticism, 18
Greg, W. W., 13
Greg-Bowers model, 13–14; challenges
to, 18; and digital editions, 21; and
European editing, 17; *Studies in
Bibliography* and, 131n10; and textual
purity, 36–37
Groden, Michael, 16
Grusin, Richard, 120, 121
Gubar, Susan, 63
Gutenberg Project, 21

Hall, Stuart, 48
Harner, James, 111
Harris, Sharon: and *Early American
Women Writers (EAWW)*, 62, 65, 78,
140n9; on technology standards, 84

Harrison, Les, 136n2
HAS-TAC, 39
Hayles, Katherine, 117
heat maps, 96, 97f
Hemings, James, 114
high literary criticism, 14
Hill, W. Speed: on digital archive, 46;
on digital edition, 22, 24
histograms, 96, 98f
historians: vs. literary editors, 30–32,
56–59. *See also* new historicism
Hockey, Susan, 2, 6, 29
Howard, Jennifer, 1
HTML (HyperText Markup Language), 65; transition away from, 83,
84, 88; and web publishing, 69
Hughes, Langston, 124
humanities: critique of, 120–21; digital
vs. traditional, 125–26. *See also* digital
humanities (dh)
humanities computing, 2–3; use of
term, 2, 3, 129n5
Humanities Computing (McCarty),
3, 6
Hume, Robert, 17
Hyperpro, 100

IATH. *See* Institute for Advanced
Technology in the Humanities
Ide, Nancy, 30
images: in digital editions, 48. *See also*
visualization
inclusivity, issue of, 51, 110
Index Thomisticus (concordance program), 2
Indiana University: and *Victorian
Women Writers Project*, 80–81; and
The Wright American Fiction dataset,
147n52
infrastructure support, and digital
project preservation, 82
Institute for Advanced Technology in
the Humanities (IATH), University
of Virginia, 42, 142n28
institutional apparatus, Foucault on,
48–49

institutional power structures, digital humanities and challenges to, 120, 122, 124–25, 127
interdisciplinarity: of digital humanities, 5, 58, 60; tensions associated with, 58–59
Internet: and canon expansion, 65, 68–69; and democratization of knowledge, 64–65. *See also* World Wide Web
The Internet Archive, 78
interpretation: data-driven approaches to, 96–102; shift from representation to, in digital literary studies, 91–92; tool development and, 9, 92–93, 94–96, 99, 100. *See also* algorithmic interpretation

Jackson, Virginia, 100
Jefferson, Thomas: digital edition of papers of, 114, 148n66; visualization of relation arcs of, 114, 115f
Jewell, Andrew: on technology standards, 84; and *The Willa Cather Archive*, 39
Jockers, Matthew L., 6, 91
The John Keats Hypermedia Archive, 87
Jones, Steven E., 6
journals, electronic, 126
JUXTA, 94, 95–96, 99, 145n17

Kichuk, Diana, 108
Kirsch, Adam, 118
Kirschenbaum, Matthew: and *Aggripa (A Book of the Dead)*, 82; on anomalies in datamining, 114; on construct vs. practice of digital humanities, 118; on democratizing effect of digital humanities, 122; on digital vs. traditional humanists, 125–26, 139n57; on efforts to define digital humanities, 2, 3; influential blog post of, 6; *Mechanisms: New Media and the Forensic Imagination*, 120; on preservation of digital projects, 87;

on stability of digital forms, 86; and UVA Etext Center, 74
Kitchen Table: Women of Color Press, 63
Klein, Lauren, 114–16, 148n66
knowledge: Internet and democratization of, 64–65; and power, 48–49
Kolko, Beth E., 62

Laden, Sonja, 46
Landow, George, 137n14
Lasseter, Janice Milner, 140n9
Levinson, Marjorie, 44, 45
libraries, etext centers in, 73–74
linguistic analysis, early digital work and, 2
literary canon: continuing controversy over, 85; digital recovery projects and expansion of, 9, 63, 65–76, 89; expansion in 1970s and 1980s, 63–64; funding priorities and, 86; Internet and expansion of, 65, 68–69; shift of focus away from, 76, 77f; technology standards and, 83–84; traditional texts in, 86, 89
literary criticism: vs. textual studies, 15–17. *See also* digital literary studies
Litz, A. Walton, 132n33
Liu, Alan: and *Aggripa (A Book of the Dead)*, 82; on anecdote, 55, 58; on digital humanities as "service," 124; influential blog post of, 6; *Romantic Chronology*, 39; *The Voice of the Shuttle (VOS)*, 71, 77–78, 141n21

MAB. *See* Medieval Academy Books
The Madwoman in the Attic (Gilbert and Gubar), 63
The Making of Americans (Stein), 105
Mandell, Laura, 74, 107–8
Mapel-Bloomberg, Kristin, 73, 140n9
Mark Twain in His Times, 141n28
Matthews, Victoria Earle, 84
McCarty, Willard, 124; Humanities Computing, 3, 6
McEntee, Gran, 140n9